Contents

Content Guidance

Questions & Answers

■Getting the most from this book

Exam tips

Advice on key points in the text to help you learn and recall content, avoid pitfalls, and polish your exam technique in order to boost your grade.

Knowledge check

Rapid-fire questions throughout the Content Guidance section to check your understanding.

Knowledge check answers

1 Turn to the back of the book for the Knowledge check answers.

Summaries

■ Each core topic is rounded off by a bullet-list summary for quick-check reference of what you need to know.

Exam-style questions

Commentary on the questions

Tips on what you need to do to gain full marks, indicated by the icon **e**

Sample student answers

Practise the questions, then look at the student answers that follow.

(d) Evaluate the extent to which you believe Sam's idea to move to team-working has been influenced by the theories of either Herzberg or Maslow. [15 marks]

e 'Evaluate' means that a judgement needs to be made, in other words an extended argument needs to be made either supporting or rejecting the view that the chosen theory can be linked with team-working. This might be achieved by looking at both sides of the argument and then drawing an overall conclusion.

(e) To what extent do you believe the introduction of team-working will lead to significant improvements in the problems in the distribution section? [15 marks]

e Although team-working is an aspect of both parts (d) and (e), they require totally different answers. The focus of this question is the problems within the distribution section of the business and an argument needs to be fully developed and in context as to whether a move to team-working will overcome the problems

Student A

(a) (i) Increase in customer complaints = $\dfrac{\text{difference between number of complaints this year and last year}}{\text{number of complaints last year}} \times 100$

(ii) Labour retention = $\dfrac{\text{number of employees employed for more than 1 year}}{\text{total number of employees}} \times 100$

(iii) Labour turnover = $\dfrac{\text{number of employees who have left during the year}}{\text{total number of employees}} \times 100$

e 6/6 marks awarded. All correct for 2 marks each.

(b) A hard approach to management is one where workers are given very little say in what they are doing and the manager tends to be autocratic in their approach. Such an approach can upset workers and lead to a lack of motivation and poor performance. This seems to be the case with the new manager who was brought into the distribution department. Although there were problems before his appointment, the increasing complaints, lower labour retention rate and rising labour turnover illustrate the likely drawbacks resulting from a hard approach to human relations.

e 5/5 marks awarded. A good answer. An understanding of a hard approach to management is demonstrated and set in the context of Gallagher's Ales.

(c) The Hackman and Oldham model looks at work from the point of view of three characteristics: the core job dimensions, the psychological states and the outcomes. Working backwards in the model, management would like the following outcomes: motivation of the workforce, improved performance, satisfaction and low absenteeism/turnover. These outcomes are more likely to be achieved if the following psychological states are present: the work is meaningful, workers have responsibility for the

76   AQA Business

Commentary on sample student answers

Find out how many marks each answer would be awarded in the exam and then read the comments (preceded by the icon **e**) following each student answer. Annotations that link back to points made in the student answers show exactly how and where marks are gained or lost.

AS/A-LEVEL YEAR 1

STUDENT GUIDE

AQA

Business

Topics 1.4–1.6

Decision-making to improve operational performance

Decision-making to improve financial performance

Decision-making to improve human resource performance

Neil James

PHILIP ALLAN FOR
HODDER
EDUCATION
AN HACHETTE UK COMPANY

Philip Allan, an imprint of Hodder Education, an Hachette UK company, Blenheim Court, George Street, Banbury, Oxfordshire OX16 5BH

Orders

Bookpoint Ltd, 130 Milton Park, Abingdon, Oxfordshire OX14 4SB

tel: 01235 827827

fax: 01235 400401

e-mail: education@bookpoint.co.uk

Lines are open 9.00 a.m.–5.00 p.m., Monday to Saturday, with a 24-hour message answering service. You can also order through the Hodder Education website: www.hoddereducation.co.uk

ISBN 978-1-4718-4423-2

First printed 2015

Impression number 5 4 3 2

Year 2019 2018 2017 2016

This Guide has been written specifically to support students preparing for the AQA AS and A-level Business (Topics 1.4–1.6) examinations. The content has been neither approved nor endorsed by AQA and remains the sole responsibility of the author.

Typeset by Integra Software Services Pvt. Ltd., Pondicherry, India

Cover photo: Giuseppe Porzani/Fotolia

Printed in Dubai

Hachette UK's policy is to use papers that are natural, renewable and recyclable products and made from wood grown in sustainable forests. The logging and manufacturing processes are expected to conform to the environmental regulations of the country of origin.

■ About this book

This Student Guide 2, together with its companion Student Guide 1, has been written with one thing in mind: to provide you with the ideal resource for your revision of both AQA AS Business (7131) and the first year of AQA A-level Business (7132). In your study of the subject you will look at business in a variety of contexts, small and large, national and global, service and manufacturing.

The overall focus of the AS Business and first year of the A-level specifications is decision-making in the various functional areas, the influences on those decisions and the impact they may have on stakeholders. Central to these specifications are the following themes:

■ How developments in technology are affecting decisions in the functional areas.
■ The influence of ethical and environmental issues on decisions in the functional areas.
■ How decision-making in the various functional areas improves competitiveness.
■ The interrelationship between decision-making in the various functional areas.

The focus of Student Guide 2 is the following:

■ Decision-making to improve operational performance — productivity and efficiency, quality and inventory and supply chains.
■ Decision-making to improve financial performance — setting objectives, analysing performance, sources of finance and improving cash flow and profit.
■ Decision-making to improve human resource performance — setting objectives, analysing performance, improving organisational design, improving motivation and improving employer–employee relations.

Content Guidance

The Content Guidance section offers concise coverage combining an overview of key terms and concepts with identification of opportunities for you to illustrate higher level skills of analysis and evaluation.

Questions & Answers

The Questions & Answers section provides examples of the various types of questions with which you are likely to be faced, such as multiple choice, short answer, data response, a case study (based on the content of both Student Guides 1 and 2) and, for A-level only, essay questions. There is also a section on quantitative skills question practice that provides additional examples of the type of calculations you are likely to be faced with. The multiple-choice and short-answer questions focus on the broad content of this guide and the three data-response questions focus on specific aspects of content. Student Guide 2 also contains a case study question that provides a much broader approach to the complete AS specification and covers content from both Student Guides 1 and 2.

The questions in this guide are tailored so that you can apply your learning while the topic is still fresh in your mind, either during the course itself or when you have revised a topic in preparation for the exam. Together with the sample answers, this should provide you with a sound basis for sitting your exams in Business.

Content Guidance

This section outlines the following areas of the AS Business and first year of the A-level Business specifications:

- Decision-making to improve operational performance
- Decision-making to improve financial performance
- Decision-making to improve human resource performance

Read through the topic area before attempting a question from the Questions & Answers section.

■ Decision-making to improve operational performance

Operations management is concerned with converting materials and labour into goods and services in the most efficient manner possible in order to maximise the profit of a business. In other words, it is about providing customers with products and services in the most efficient way possible.

Setting operational objectives

Operations management turns inputs into outputs with the aim of adding value, which is essential for a business to make a profit. The value of the output (product or service) should be greater than the value of the inputs needed to produce it. **Added value** is the difference between the price of a finished product or service and the cost of the inputs involved in making it. Adding value is therefore one of a number of aims of operations management.

Operations management is no different to other functional areas in that it has its own set of objectives, which will be SMART. The attainment of these objectives leads a business towards achieving its overall business long-term goals. Further examples of operational objectives are:

- **Costs** — this is usually in terms of unit cost of production. Lower unit costs can lead to a competitive advantage as long as other objectives are not compromised such as quality and environmental objectives. Examples of objectives related to the area of cost and efficiency include productivity, unit cost of production and capacity utilisation.
- **Quality** — this refers not only to the final product or service but also to the whole process of producing and selling that product or service. Objectives in this area might be in regard to wastage, defect rates, reliability and customer complaints.
- **Speed of response and flexibility** — this relates to how quickly a business can respond to changes in demand, and effectiveness in this area has a significant impact on efficiency and unit costs. An example of an objective here might be in terms of order lead times.

Added value The amount added to the value of a product or service, made up of the difference between the cost of producing it and the amount received when it is sold.

Exam tip

It is not only operations management that adds value, marketing can also.

Lead times The time it takes from ordering stock to when the order is received by the customer.

- **Dependability** — this is the reliability of the business, which is essential in maintaining customer loyalty.
- **Environmental objectives** — this has become increasingly important over recent years where objectives relating to the amount of packaging used, energy efficiency, waste disposal and the use of sustainable resources have become an important area of concern.

The value of setting operational objectives

Operational objectives are important for a business for a number of reasons:

- They promote efficiency and can make savings in terms of time, money and less waste.
- Unit costs may be reduced as a result of the efficiencies gained.
- Profitability is therefore likely to improve.
- Motivation may be gained for those responsible for achieving the objectives set.
- Evaluation of the objectives set may be used as a measure of achievement.

External and internal influences on operational objectives and decisions

Operations managers do not operate in isolation. Any decisions made will have implications for the other functional areas of the business and may be affected by the wider external environment.

External

External influences usually involve the following factors.

Political or legal influences

Businesses always have to be aware of the legal environment and potential changes in legislation. With greater awareness of health and safety and environmental issues, changes to legislation in these areas could have a significant impact on operational objectives.

Economic influences

Changes in the economic environment can impact on operational objectives as demand is likely to fluctuate with changes in the economic cycle. Added to this is the effect of greater globalisation, which enables businesses to source both supplies and produce from almost anywhere in the world.

Technological influences

This has had a tremendous effect on both the way consumers purchase goods and services and in terms of production. The advent of the internet has led to consumers who are more aware and demanding in terms of price, quality and customer service. There are apps for just about anything and the growth of social media influences operations objectives. Not only has technology influenced consumer awareness, it has also had a profound impact on the production of goods and services. Production can be undertaken with the use of robots, the process of innovation is quicker, books and newspapers can be read online and music and films simply streamed or downloaded.

> **Knowledge check 2**
> Outline briefly how environmental concerns have an impact on operational objectives.

> **Knowledge check 3**
> Identify four reasons why it is important for a business to set operational objectives.

> **Globalisation**
> The tendency of businesses to move beyond domestic and national markets to other markets around the globe, thereby increasing the interconnectedness of markets and business.

Competitive influences

Greater awareness means a business has to work hard to maintain customer loyalty. This places pressure on operations to maintain levels of quality, reliability and customer service.

Internal

Internal influences are usually studied in terms of other functional areas:

- **Finance** — as any operational decision is likely to involve considerable investment, the availability of finance is a key influence.
- **Marketing** — it may be that the marketing activities of a business determine the quantities produced and the type of good manufactured.
- **Human resources** — it is likely that the skills of the workforce determine the quality and numbers produced. This emphasises the importance of the workforce.

As well as the above, the overall corporate objectives are also likely to influence operational objectives.

> **Corporate objectives** The overall business objectives that influence strategic decision-making and to which each functional area (operations management, finance, marketing and human resources) will work towards.

Analysing operational performance

Interpretation of operations data

As with other objectives, operational objectives should be measurable, enabling managers to analyse and interpret the results. Four main areas are outlined in the AQA specification:

- labour productivity
- unit cost (average cost)
- capacity
- capacity utilisation

We will look at each of these areas in turn.

> **Productivity** A measure of the efficiency of a person, machine, factory, etc. in converting inputs into useful output.

Calculation of operations data

Labour productivity

This relates to the efficiency of individual workers and is of interest to human resources as well as operational managers. It is a measure of the output per worker in a given time period and calculated as follows:

$$\text{Labour productivity} = \frac{\text{output per time period}}{\text{number of employees}}$$

Therefore, if an output of 3,000 units is achieved in a given time period by 25 workers, the labour productivity is 120.

Unit cost (average cost)

This is the cost of producing one unit of output and is sometimes referred to as average cost of production. It is calculated as follows:

$$\text{Unit cost} = \frac{\text{total cost of production}}{\text{output}}$$

Therefore, if the total cost of producing 3,000 units of output is £90,000, the unit cost is £30.

Capacity

This refers to the maximum output possible for a business in a given time period. Using the example above, although production is 3,000 units it may be possible for a business to produce 4,000 units in the same time period. Therefore, 4,000 units is its maximum capacity. However, there is no point in producing at this level unless demand is there as this would incur unnecessary costs.

Capacity utilisation

Capacity refers to the total possible production in a given time period, but capacity utilisation measures what percentage of that capacity is actually used. It is calculated as follows:

$$\text{Capacity utilisation} = \frac{\text{actual output per time period}}{\text{maximum possible output per time period}} \times 100$$

In the example above, if maximum capacity is 4,000 units and actual output is 3,000 units, capacity utilisation is 75%.

The use of data in operational decision-making and planning

Data can be useful in making operational decisions and, with the greater use of technology, they can be easier and quicker to identify and collect. The analysis of operational data enables problems to be spotted at an early stage. This might be in terms of productivity, unit costs or capacity utilisation. If demand is shown to be increasing, it may be necessary to find some way of increasing capacity to avoid problems of lack of capacity. If unit costs are increasing, an analysis of why may enable corrective action to be taken. If an early indication of falling productivity is shown, it may be possible to take corrective action before it becomes a real problem.

Operational data are likely to be a starting point for any operational decisions that are made and therefore have an important role to play in decision-making.

Opportunities for analysis

- The importance of operational objectives.
- Analysis of either internal or external factors that may be considered when setting operational objectives.

Opportunities for evaluation

- Evaluation of whether internal or external factors might be more important in a given context.
- The extent to which one operational objective might be the most important in a given context.
- Evaluation of the usefulness of operations data.

Exam tip

It is relatively easy to calculate unit cost for a business producing a single product, but more difficult for a multi-product firm.

Knowledge check 4

Distinguish between capacity and capacity utilisation.

Making operational decisions to improve performance: increasing efficiency and productivity

Operational efficiency is defined as the ratio between the inputs to run a business and the outputs gained. The aim is to achieve the greatest amount of outputs from the lowest amount of inputs without compromising other aspects such as quality or customer service.

The importance of capacity

It is important for a business to have the right level of capacity. If it has too much spare or excess capacity it is not using, this represents wasted resources as it will be paying for space it is not using which will have an impact on unit cost. If, however, it is operating at full capacity, the business will be unable to take on new orders and could miss out on valuable sales and may even damage its reputation.

How to utilise capacity efficiently

Capacity utilisation in the UK averaged 72.11% from 1958 to 2014 and was at its highest (85.2%) in 1988. Ideally, a business requires a level of capacity utilisation as close to 100% as possible but in practice this is unlikely for most firms. However, having some spare capacity is advisable as this gives the business the flexibility to be able to take on new orders. For some businesses, demand may be seasonal, resulting in working flat-out at certain times of year while having spare capacity at other times. An individual business, therefore, will be aware of its optimal and most efficient level of capacity utilisation and aims to operate at this level.

The importance of efficiency and labour productivity

The efficiency of a business might be improved by increasing labour productivity, i.e. the output per worker. This might be achieved by getting a greater output from the existing workforce in the same time period, but this requires a market and demand for the extra output. On the other hand, it might be achieved by producing the same level of output from a smaller workforce. In both cases, the cost of labour per unit is reduced (assuming labour costs do not change). Labour productivity is a key figure particularly in businesses that rely on a high proportion of labour in production. Improvements in productivity have a significant impact on efficiency.

How to increase efficiency and labour productivity

Labour productivity can be improved in a number of ways:

- **Reduce the labour force.** If the labour force can be reduced while maintaining the same level of production, productivity will improve. This could be achieved by investing in technology or sub-contracting some peripheral activities such as cleaning.
- **Invest in technology.** Many operations in manufacturing are undertaken by machines and robots. In the service industry, examples such as online banking reduce the need for labour, thereby improving the productivity of the remaining staff.

Exam tip

When looking at capacity utilisation, it is important to look at the circumstances of the individual business. Has its capacity utilisation been rising or falling? How has it performed against an industry average? Any judgement made must be in context.

Knowledge check 5

What do you understand by the term 'excess capacity'?

- **Improve training and motivation.** Increasing the skill set of workers may make them more efficient and, if this is linked to motivation and reward, productivity may be improved.
- **Job redesign.** This can also have an impact on productivity as changing the way things are done can make the whole process more efficient.

Difficulties of increasing efficiency and labour productivity

Although improving labour productivity might seem a straightforward aim in practice, it can lead to significant difficulties:

- **Quality.** Increasing the output per worker may compromise other factors such as the quality of a product or service.
- **Resistance of employees.** Productivity increases may be resisted by employees as it may result in redundancies. This is not just as a result of new technology being introduced — it could also happen if productivity is improved with no corresponding increase in demand.
- **Costs.** It is also possible that workers may demand pay increases in recognition of their improved performance or to reward new skills developed through training.

The benefits and difficulties of lean production

Lean production is about getting more from less. It involves eliminating waste and involves, where possible, using less labour, materials, space and time. It is about making the organisation more efficient and, in turn, reducing costs. There are perhaps four aspects of lean production:

- **Just-in-time (JIT) production**, where materials are received just as they are needed for production, eliminating the need for large levels of stock.
- **Time-based management**, which aims to reduce the time wasted in operations, such as in faster product development and shorter lead times.
- **Total quality management (TQM)**, which is a quality assurance ideal where all workers have responsibility for getting it right first time. (See p. 14 for more information on quality assurance.)
- **Continuous improvement**, which is a culture where all workers are involved in making improvements in production and quality.

Lean production can be applied to both manufacturing and the service sector and it brings with it a number of efficiency benefits. These include improved productivity, reduced waste and improved customer service.

The AQA specification makes specific reference to just-in-time operations, where materials are received as they are required for production or needed for sale. Such a system places a greater responsibility on employees, not just for ordering and ensuring sufficient materials arrive but also in terms of flexibility in adjusting to variable levels of demand. There are a number of benefits of using just-in-time:

- **Reduced costs**. Less space is needed for storage, less workers are required for looking after stock and there is less wastage due to damaged stock. Less money is tied up in holding stock, so the business's cash flow position is likely to be improved.

Knowledge check 6

List four ways in which labour productivity may be improved.

Exam tip

Whether or not productivity improvements can be made effectively depends on the circumstances of the individual firm and the costs involved.

Lean production This is about getting more from less. It focuses on cutting out waste in terms of labour, materials, space and time.

Just-in-time (JIT) A strategy that some companies employ in order to increase efficiency and decrease waste by receiving goods only as they are needed in the production process, thereby reducing inventory costs.

- **Greater motivation**. There is greater worker participation in decision-making and jobs are likely to be more interesting and carry more responsibility as a result.

There are a number of drawbacks in adopting a lean production approach:

- **Loss of production**. If there is any interruption in the supply chain, materials may not arrive on time. This might be because of weather disruption or problems in the supplier's production process. This was illustrated when a tsunami struck Japan in March 2011, destroying many supplier firms to the car industry. As a result, Toyota had to halt production for a number of months.
- **Reliability and flexibility**. Tremendous trust is put in suppliers by such a system. This is not just based on their ability to supply reliably and be flexible, but also for being able to produce consistently high quality.
- **Bulk purchase savings**. These may not be available as each order will be for a small quantity.

How to choose the optimal mix of resources

The inputs needed in business are often referred to as the *factors of production*. These are the resources used in the production of goods and services. They include:

- land — the physical land and the natural resources of the planet
- labour — the staff that work in a business
- capital — the machines and equipment used in a business
- enterprise — the skill of combining the other factors of production

When considering the optimum use of resources, it is usually in relation to the mix of capital and labour. Some businesses may put a great emphasis on capital (*capital intensive*), whereas others place more emphasis on labour (*labour intensive*).

The car industry provides an example of a capital-intensive industry where large amounts of money have been invested in technology and robots for the mass production of cars. This brings with it the benefits of higher productivity and efficiency in terms of reducing human error and wastage. It does, however, come with a high initial cost and, unlike labour, lacks flexibility and creativity.

An example of a labour-intensive organisation is a restaurant or hotel that is heavily reliant on customer service. Its staff can be used flexibly according to demand: they can tailor-make products, add personal touches and give feedback on production. Along with labour, however, comes the potential for labour-relation problems: their effort can be inconsistent, long term they can be more expensive and there may be problems acquiring labour with the correct skills.

The optimal mix of resources depends on a number of factors:

- **The type of product being made**. Mass-produced products are likely to be more capital intensive, whereas those aimed at a niche market may be more labour intensive, for example Nissan cars as opposed to Aston Martin.
- **The size of the business and finance available**. Smaller businesses may not be able to justify investment into large items of capital equipment.
- **The nature of the industry.** The service industry such as the hotel trade is more likely to be labour intensive as customer service is paramount. On the other hand, manufacturing is more likely to be capital intensive.

Exam tip

It may be that a business will not lose out from not buying in bulk. This is because through the course of a year they are likely to still order the same amount and, theoretically, the supplier should also benefit from a lower requirement for storage space.

Knowledge check 7

Outline two benefits and two drawbacks of a just-in-time approach to production.

Knowledge check 8

Distinguish between capital-intensive and labour-intensive production.

How to use technology to improve operational efficiency

Technological developments have had a significant impact on all aspects of business, research and development, production and sales. This influence has been apparent in every sector, making operations more efficient. We have computer-aided design (CAD) and computer-aided manufacture (CAM), which make innovation quicker and manufacture more accurate, reducing wastage and improving quality.

Computers enable quicker communication and large amounts of data to be stored and processed. Goods and services can be purchased on the internet at the touch of a button. Information can be spread via social media in an instant. Technology also continues to develop, enabling further efficiencies to be achieved. Providing a business has the finance to invest and the skills to use the technology, the benefits in terms of efficiency are enormous:

- Cost reduction — this can be in manufacturing due to less waste, speedier production and the use of less labour. It can also be in the service sector in terms of online sales, reducing the need for high street shops and sales assistants.
- Flexibility — this might be in production, for example car manufacturers can build cars specifically to meet customer requirements in terms of colour and extras.
- Innovation — this may be quicker, resulting in new products becoming available sooner.

Opportunities for analysis

- The factors that might be considered when deciding to move from capital-intensive to labour-intensive production.
- Analysis of the benefits or drawbacks of just-in-time production.
- Analysis of the methods of improving productivity.

Opportunities for evaluation

- The extent to which moving to a capital-intensive production approach is appropriate.
- Evaluation of the benefits of technology.
- The extent to which a just-in-time approach to production benefits a business.

Making operational decisions to improve performance: improving quality

Quality is a measure of excellence — the state of a product or service being free from defects, deficiencies and significant variation. It requires a consistent commitment to set standards to satisfy consumer requirements.

The importance of quality

Most businesses operate in a competitive environment, which means that consumers have a choice when it comes to the purchase of a good or service. As a result, businesses look to gain a competitive advantage, which means that consumers choose

Exam tip

Some businesses might put greater emphasis on aspects other than quality — such as price — and attempt to gain a competitive advantage through value for money rather than overall quality.

povler

to buy their product or service over others that are available. Having a high quality product or service is one way of achieving this. Quality might be in the form of:

- the reliability of the product or service
- the customer service provided, including after-sales service
- having a superior product or service

The importance of quality is in creating a happy consumer who, having purchased a product or service once, will have no hesitation in purchasing again or recommending to friends and family. A business may therefore aim for 'quality this time, next time and every time'.

Methods of improving quality

A manufacturing business might use the following measures of quality:

- amount of wastage
- number of returns
- number of complaints

In the service sector, further measures such as punctuality and time taken to serve a customer could be used.

Targets for improvements in any of these areas might therefore be set in an attempt to improve the overall quality of a product or service. The main methods used for improving quality and achieving targets would be through a *quality control* system or a **quality assurance** system. There is no requirement in the AQA specification for an understanding of quality control, but it is worth outlining and comparing with quality assurance, which is required.

Quality control involves physical inspection by a quality controller to check both materials received and completed work. Such a system aims to prevent faulty goods reaching the consumer.

Quality assurance, on the other hand, is the responsibility of all workers. It occurs throughout the production process and is concerned with trying to stop faults happening in order to achieve zero defects. With all staff responsible for this system, quality should be more consistent with less wastage and greater involvement and motivation of the workforce. There are a number of ways of achieving quality assurance:

- **Kaizen** is a Japanese business philosophy based on making positive changes on a regular basis. It means continuous improvement and is one of Toyota's core values in production. In practice, it means that all team members in all parts of the business are continuously looking for ways to improve operations. This results in a culture that encourages participation and involvement.
- **Total quality management (TQM)** occurs where there is a culture of quality running through the organisation and involving the whole workforce. Its aim is to get it right first time.

Underlying these methods of improving quality is having the right attitude and having the commitment to quality while giving employees the skills and freedom to participate in the quality process.

E: person/HAT
IHandy Entrepreneur

The benefits and difficulties of improving quality

Improving quality can bring with it a number of benefits:

- Increased sales because of an enhanced reputation, which should lead to greater revenue and profit.
- Lower costs as a result of less wastage and returns.
- A unique selling point (USP) may be established as a result of high quality. Sony and VW have established reputations and brand images of quality. This may mean higher prices can be charged and justified.
- A competitive advantage, which enhances the business's reputation and creates consumer brand loyalty.

Improving quality seems easy in theory, but in practice it may be difficult to implement. There are a number of obstacles that need to be overcome:

- The attitude of employees is important as they can be resistant to change. They may not believe there is a problem and may see any changes as a threat to job security. If their responsibilities are increased, they may seek a higher reward. This, and the costs of any training needed, may prove too expensive.
- There may be problems with finance because improving quality does not come without some financial cost. The cost of training and the technology required can be high.

The consequences of poor quality

If a business does not address the issues of poor quality, there could be far-reaching and damaging consequences:

- Sales — poor quality is likely to have an impact on sales as consumers might purchase a product once but they would be unlikely to repeat purchase. This affects sales volumes, sales revenue and, ultimately, profit.
- Costs — these are in terms of waste, returned products and extra time spent on administration and repair. As a result, unit costs may begin to increase.
- Reputation — it takes a long time to establish a reputation but it can be destroyed overnight. Once a business is known for poor quality, it takes a long time to convince customers otherwise.
- Waste — this is not just in terms of materials and poor quality products but also in time and space. As sales decline, so will capacity utilisation. Assets are not used efficiently and labour may become idle, resulting in layoffs and potential labour-relation problems.

In the competitive global environment that exists today, a business ignores quality at its peril.

Opportunities for analysis

- Analysis of the benefits of good quality or the problems of poor quality.
- Analysis of the factors that might be considered before introducing a quality assurance system.
- Analysis of the difficulties in improving quality.

Opportunities for evaluation

- Evaluation of the extent to which improvement in quality is the most important operational objective.

Exam tip

TQM should not be viewed as a separate approach from Kaizen; Kaizen can be seen as part of a TQM process.

Knowledge check 11

Why might the attitude of employees cause difficulties in improving quality?

Knowledge check 12

Explain why 'a business ignores quality issues at its peril'.

Making operational decisions to improve performance: managing inventory and supply chains

Inventory is the business term used for stock. A business might hold inventory in the form of materials for production, materials that are in the process of being produced (work in progress) or finished products. The **supply chain** encompasses the steps it takes to get a good or service from the supplier to the consumer. Supply chain activities transform natural resources, raw materials and components into finished products that are delivered to consumers.

Ways and value of improving flexibility, speed of response and dependability

When buying a product, consumers — whether business to business (B2B) or business to consumer (B2C) — look for the following characteristics.

Flexibility

The ability to be flexible may give a business a significant advantage, whether it is a supplier who is prepared to accept varying orders rather than a set order each month or a manufacturer who is able to tailor production to a consumer's exact requirements. The process of tailoring a product to consumer requirements is known as **mass customisation** and is now apparent in many industries. For example, when buying paint it can be mixed in the shop to give an exact match to a consumer's sample and when buying a car a consumer can effectively build their own in terms of colour and accessories. Again, closer links with suppliers and improvements in communication and technology may be the key to improvements in flexibility.

Speed of response

This is closely linked to dependability as consumers require and expect a quick response to any order or request. Again, closer relationships and improved communication technology are likely to lead to improvements.

Dependability/reliability

Dependability relates to the idea that a business starts and finishes a particular job at a set time. Whether it is the supply of materials, the supply of a finished product or the provision of a service, it is essential that things happen at the appointed time. Any disruption has implications for the business. If supplies do not arrive on time, production may be delayed; if a consumer does not receive goods on time, business reputation may be damaged; if an installation of new equipment is delayed, production may be disrupted. Therefore, dependability is important as any breakdown could have significant cost implications. It might be improved by establishing closer relationships with supplier companies, for example working with them in developing new products and components. The introduction of communication technology might also enhance relations and make them more dependable as a result.

Inventory Also known as stock, this is the goods or materials that a business holds for the ultimate purpose of resale or repair.

Supply chain The network of businesses involved in getting a product or service to the consumer. In manufacturing, for example, the supply chain includes sellers of raw materials, manufacturers, wholesalers and retailers.

Mass customisation A marketing and manufacturing technique that combines the flexibility of personalisation that comes with custom-made goods with the low unit costs associated with mass production.

Exam tip

Whether a business needs to make improvements in these areas depends on the nature of the business. In producing a luxury car such as an Aston Martin, speed of response may not be that crucial but flexibility might in terms of colour and accessories.

How to manage supply to match demand and the value of doing so

A business wishes to maximise its sales and key to this is matching supply to demand. If it runs out of stock and cannot satisfy demand sales, revenue and potential profit are lost. If it produces too much, there will be costs associated with storage and wastage, reducing potential profit. There are a number of ways in which an operations manager might match supply to demand:

- **Flexible workforce**. This might be achieved by employing part-time or temporary staff or by employing staff on zero-hours contracts. This way, employment can be increased easily to cope with sudden increases in demand. Similarly, having a workforce that is multi-skilled may enable the business to cope with fluctuations in demand.
- **Increase capacity**. This might be a long-term solution if any increase in demand is seen to be permanent rather than a temporary or seasonal variation.
- **Produce to order**. This is where a business produces a product only when an order has been received. Examples of this are tailor-made suits, aeroplane construction or a meal in a restaurant. It would not be suitable for every business and requires a skilled and flexible workforce.
- **Outsource production**. Also sometimes called sub-contracting, this is where another business is tasked with producing products. Although outsourcing enables a business to satisfy demand quickly, it does have some problems. (See p. 19 for more information on outsourcing.)

great speed of response

Influences on the amount of inventory held

Inventory refers to the stock held by a business and it is important in order to ensure that customer orders may be satisfied quickly and efficiently. There are a number of influences on the amount of inventory held:

- **Nature of the product**. A business does not want to hold large amounts of perishable items as they may quickly deteriorate and be wasted. Neither does it want to hold large amounts of products that have short product life cycles as they could quickly become out of date.
- **Nature of demand**. The demand for some products may be seasonal in nature or variable because of the weather. Businesses try to anticipate this variability and hold sufficient stock in order to be able to satisfy demand.
- **Opportunity cost**. Any stock held represents money tied up and so could present an opportunity cost. In other words, it might be more beneficial to employ that money elsewhere in the business.

It is important that inventory is managed carefully and therefore an inventory control chart might be used, as shown in Figure 1. The features of this chart include:

- Buffer inventory — the minimum amount of inventory (stock) that a business wants to hold. This is to cover for emergencies such as supplies not arriving on time or a sudden and unexpected increase in demand.
- Reorder level — the level at which a new order for stock is made and depends on the lead time and buffer inventory.

Knowledge check 13

Distinguish between buffer inventory, reorder level and reorder quantity.

■ Lead time — the time it takes from the order being placed to actual delivery of stock. The lead time determines when an order has to be placed in order to prevent the stock level going below the buffer inventory.

■ Reorder quantity — the amount that is reordered at any particular time.

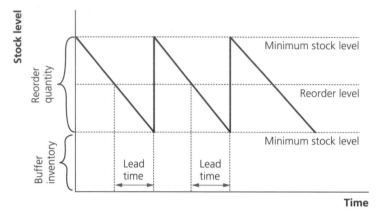

Figure 1 An inventory control chart

The key to having an effective inventory control system is that orders are made and supplied on time and that demand is predictable.

Influences on the choice of suppliers

When deciding on which supplier to use, the operations manager considers a number of factors:

■ Quality — a business does not want to compromise its own standards by using poor quality, unreliable materials and components from suppliers.

■ Cost — this in itself may not be an issue as a business wants the right price for the quality of product it is receiving. It wants value for money. Payment terms, however, may be an important factor as a longer payment period may help its cash flow.

■ Dependability — a business wants reliable suppliers who deliver when they say they will.

■ Flexibility — if demand is variable, having suppliers who can be flexible may be an important consideration.

■ Ethics — with greater consumer awareness regarding a business's social responsibility, ethical issues have become increasingly important.

How to manage the supply chain effectively and efficiently and the value of this

The supply chain encompasses the steps it takes to get a good or service from the supplier to the consumer and includes the providers of materials, components, finance and people. In order to manage this effectively, it is necessary for managers to make decisions in terms of what and how much to produce and which suppliers to use. These decisions are influenced by a number of internal and external factors:

Exam tip

The relative importance of any one factor depends on the individual business and the clues to this are contained in any stimulus material provided. Read it carefully and apply the information effectively.

- Internally, the supply chain is influenced by forecasts produced by the marketing department; the financial procedures, policies and finance available; and the corporate and associated functional objectives set.
- Externally, the supply chain is influenced by the dependability of the supplier and quality of product and service. Ethical issues are increasingly also taken into consideration.

These internal and external factors are considered in order to manage the supply chain with the aim of getting the right supplies in the right place at the right time. If this can be achieved, it enables the business to maximise sales while avoiding criticism from pressure groups for using suppliers that employ child labour in sweatshops or scandals such as the use of horse meat in products for human consumption.

The value of outsourcing

There are a number of advantages of outsourcing to an outside supplier:

- *Speed of response*. Outsourcing may enable a business to respond quickly to changes in demand, especially if they have established good relations with an outsourcing firm.
- *Saving costs*. Where capacity is limited but demand insufficient to warrant the investment in extra capacity, outsourcing may be the ideal solution, saving on investment costs while generating additional revenue and profit.
- *Core activities*. A business may see itself as being innovative and creative and wishes to focus on this aspect rather than the actual production process.

if company has 100% utilisation = costs instead of expanding production.

However, outsourcing is not the solution for every business:

- *Quality*. The outsourcing firm may not have the same high standards, which could lead to a damaged reputation.
- *Costs*. Outsourcing may be costly and this cost has to be evaluated against the benefits.
- *Trade secrets*. The business may have to allow the outsourcing company access to confidential information regarding a product or service.

Knowledge check 14

Outline the benefits and drawbacks of outsourcing.

Opportunities for analysis

- Analysis of the factors that might be considered when choosing a supplier.
- Analysis of the factors that might be considered when deciding the levels of inventory to hold.
- Analysis of the factors that might be considered before deciding to outsource production.

Opportunities for evaluation

- The extent to which improvements in operational efficiency might improve competiveness.
- Evaluation of the importance of technology in reaching operational targets.
- The extent to which price might be the most important factor when choosing a supplier.

Summary

- The value and nature of operational objectives including costs, quality, speed of response, flexibility, dependability, environmental objectives and added value.
- The calculation and interpretation of the following operational data, labour productivity, unit costs, capacity and capacity utilisation.
- The importance of using capacity efficiently.
- The importance of methods of improving and difficulties of improving labour productivity.
- The benefits and difficulties of introducing lean production with specific reference to just in time production.
- The optimal mix of resources, capital-intensive versus labour-intensive production.
- How technology might be used to improve operational performance.
- The importance of and methods of improving quality: quality control and quality assurance.
- The benefits of good quality and the consequences of poor quality.
- Inventory and the supply chain.
- Ways of improving flexibility, speed of response and dependability.
- How to match supply with demand.
- Inventory control charts and their construction.
- How to manage the supply chain effectively and the benefits of doing so.
- The value and problems of outsourcing.

◼ Decision-making to improve financial performance

Financial performance means measuring the results of a business's policies and operations in monetary terms. It examines how a business might make decisions to improve its financial position.

Setting financial objectives

The aim of most businesses is to make money (profit), but financial objectives may also determine the amount of money needed, the time frame in which it must be made and how it will be spent. Objectives in this area are influenced by the overall corporate objectives and coordinated with the other functional areas. Financial objectives are goals or targets set by the finance function of a business. They are likely to have a numerical (measurable) element and a time scale (time-based) element, as well as being specific and realistic. Possible areas for financial objectives include:

- return on capital employed (return on investment)
- cash flow targets
- profit and shareholder returns
- cost minimisation

The value of setting financial objectives

There are a number of benefits that illustrate the value of setting financial targets:

- They act as a focus for decision-making and so may enable greater coordination and efficiency. For example, it might be possible to spot potential problems at an early stage, enabling some form of corrective action to be devised and implemented.
- They provide a yardstick against which the success or failure of a business may be judged.
- Shareholders may be able to assess whether an investment is worthwhile.
- Outside organisations, particularly suppliers, may be able to judge the financial viability of a business.

The distinction between cash flow and profit

Cash flow relates to the money flowing into and out of a business. The rate at which money flows into and out of a business requires careful observation and analysis. The last thing a business wants to do is run out of cash as this could threaten its whole existence. Having finance (cash) readily available for day-to-day expenditure is essential. Generally, businesses have to pay for resources (e.g. materials and labour) long before they have made any sales and need cash for this. New orders mean greater revenue in the future, but a business must have the cash available to purchase resources in the first place. Short term, therefore, cash is essential for the very survival of a business.

Profit is the reward for taking the risk of setting up in business and is calculated as follows:

Profit = revenue − total costs

> **Knowledge check 15**
>
> Identify three benefits of setting financial objectives.

> **Cash flow** The amount of money that flows into and out of a business over a period of time.

> **Profit** The reward the owners of a business receive for taking the risk of setting up in business.

It is the money left over after all costs have been taken from the money achieved from sales (revenue). Profit or the potential for future profit is essential for the long-term survival of a business. In the short term it is possible to survive without making a profit, for example during the first few years of existence or in periods of economic downturn businesses may incur losses, but providing there is confidence in the long-term potential of the business it may be able to survive.

The distinction between gross profit, operating profit and profit for the year

Profit may be looked at in a number of different ways.

Gross profit

Gross profit is the difference between the revenue and the direct costs of producing a good or service and is calculated by subtracting the direct costs of sales from the sales revenue

The **gross profit margin** is expressed as a percentage and calculated using the following formula:

$$\text{Gross profit margin} = \frac{\text{gross profit}}{\text{sales revenue}} \times 100$$

This is more useful than just a figure for gross profit as it enables more meaningful analysis and can be compared to previous years or other businesses.

Operating profit

When calculating gross profit, only the direct costs of producing a good or service are taken into consideration. Operating profit is calculated by subtracting all the costs of producing the good or service from the sales revenue. The additional costs here are often referred to as expenses and include such things as administrative costs, directors' salaries and marketing expenses.

The **operating profit margin** is expressed as a percentage and calculated using the following formula:

$$\text{Operating profit margin} = \frac{\text{operating profit}}{\text{sales revenue}} \times 100$$

Operating profit margin can be used to make comparisons with past years and can give an indication of how well a business is controlling expenses. It can also be compared with other businesses.

Profit for the year

When calculating operating profit, certain items are not included such as interest charges, taxes on profit, any interest received or income from any investments. Therefore, profit for the year takes into consideration all income received and all costs incurred and is the final profit figure. In a public limited company the board of directors decides how much to retain in the business and how much to give to shareholders by way of a dividend.

Knowledge check 16

Distinguish between cash flow and profit.

Gross profit margin
A profitability ratio that measures how much of every pound is left over after paying the direct costs of the goods sold.

Operating profit margin
A profitability ratio that measures how much of every pound is left over after paying both the direct costs and expenses of production.

Exam tip

It is possible for gross profit to increase but operating profit to decline and an understanding of why this might happen is important.

Knowledge check 17

Explain briefly how it is possible for gross profit to stay the same while operating profit increases.

Revenue, costs and profit objectives

As part of its financial objectives, a business sets specific targets for revenue, costs and profit. These targets are influenced by the overall corporate objectives and have to be carefully coordinated with the other functional areas. For example, it might be difficult to increase revenue significantly if operations lack the capacity to increase production or the marketing department lacks the resources to increase a marketing campaign.

- **Revenue**. Revenue targets need careful consideration as many markets are highly competitive making increased revenue difficult to achieve. However, in a growing market or for a new business, a revenue target may be useful for both focusing decision-making and assessing performance.
- **Cost**. In a competitive market it may be difficult to achieve improved profit using revenue objectives as the costs associated with generating greater revenue (for example, marketing) may outweigh the benefits. In these circumstances, focusing on cost reduction may provide an alternative approach to greater profit. Retailers such as Aldi and Lidl have achieved greater revenue and profit through a policy of reduced costs.
- **Profit**. Profit targets may be illustrated in a number of ways such as a figure, a percentage or an improved margin. A figure on its own means little, but a percentage increase or improvement in profit margin can be more easily compared to other businesses in order to make a better assessment of overall performance.

Cash flow objectives

Cash flow is essential for the survival of a business. The idea that 'cash is king' rings true for many businesses as without it they can quickly become insolvent (unable to pay their way). As a result, cash flow targets might focus on one or more of the following:

- reducing the time taken for customers to pay
- increasing the credit period allowed by suppliers
- reducing borrowings and/or interest charges
- reducing seasonal swings in cash flow

Objectives for investment (capital expenditure) levels

Before looking at capital investment targets, it might be worth distinguishing between capital and revenue expenditure. Capital expenditure is money spent on long-term investment into a business such as expenditure on fixed assets like buildings and equipment. Revenue expenditure is money spent on the day-to-day running of a business such as the purchase of raw materials.

Capital expenditure is necessary in a business for a number of reasons such as financing growth through the purchase of new buildings and equipment or updating existing assets such as computer systems, machinery and equipment (necessary in order to maintain competitiveness). On the other hand, it may be required to finance the development of new assets such as a new drug for a pharmaceutical company or a new oil field for an oil company. Targets set for capital expenditure therefore depend on the type of business and the market in which it operates. The state of the economy and the financial position of a business are also likely to affect a business's capital expenditure.

Exam tip

The focus of any cash flow targets vary from business to business and their individual circumstances. As a result, it is essential to look at the circumstances of the individual business.

Knowledge check 18

Distinguish between capital and revenue expenditure.

Linked to the idea of capital investment targets is the concept of **return on investment**. This can be measured using the amount of profit generated from the investment and is calculated as follows:

$$\text{Return on investment} = \frac{\text{net profit}}{\text{amount invested}} \times 100$$

A business could therefore set a certain percentage as a target or use this when comparing a number of potential investments.

Capital structure objectives

The capital structure of a business refers to the way in which a business has raised its long-term finance. There are two key sources of long-term funding for a business — borrowing and share capital — and the relationship between these is important. This is because money that has been borrowed attracts interest payments and has to be paid back, whereas share capital does not have to be paid back and investors receive only a return (dividend) from any profit. The relationship between borrowing and equity can be measured and is known as **capital gearing**. It is expressed as a percentage and calculated using the following formula:

$$\text{Capital gearing} = \frac{\text{loan capital (borrowing)}}{\text{total capital employed (borrowing + equity)}} \times 100$$

The higher the figure, the greater the dependence on borrowing. A figure of over 50% indicates a highly geared company that might be at risk should interest rates increase. Targets may therefore be set for reducing gearing.

External and internal influences on financial objectives and decisions

There are a number of external and internal influences on financial objectives.

External influences
- **Market factors**. Whether the market is growing or declining has a big impact. For example, it would be difficult to improve profit margins in a declining market.
- **Actions of other businesses**. Competitors are likely to have an impact, particularly if they can gain first-mover advantage with a more innovative product or service.
- **PEST analysis**. This refers to the political, economic, social and technological influences on a business. Changes in legislation could result in increasing costs, changes in the economy such as increased interest rates will increase costs, and social and technological changes may result in falling sales because of changes in fashion or new improved products. All of these factors are likely to affect the ability of a business to achieve its financial targets.

Internal influences
- **Overall corporate objectives**. This may have an impact on financial objectives. For example, if an overall objective is growth, the directors may be willing to accept a higher level of gearing and a lower level of profit margin in order to achieve this.
- **Operational factors**. To some extent these can influence financial targets. For example, the ability to achieve greater profit may be limited by operational capacity.

Return on investment a performance measure used to evaluate the efficiency of an investment or to compare the efficiency of a number of different investments.

Capital gearing A financial ratio that compares borrowed funds to total capital employed (equity + borrowing).

Knowledge check 19

Explain briefly why it may be important for a business to control its capital gearing ratio.

Exam tip

A high gearing ratio is not necessarily bad if interest rates are relatively low and a business can easily service the interest payments from profit.

- **Resources available**. This includes both finance and human resources, which may limit the extent to which a business can improve profitability.

Opportunities for analysis

- Analysis of the factors that might be considered when setting financial objectives.
- Analysis of the factors that might be considered when investigating a company's profit margins.

Opportunities for evaluation

- Evaluation of whether cash flow or profit is more important to a business.
- The extent to which external or internal factors may be most important when setting financial objectives.

Analysing financial performance

How to construct and analyse budgets and cash flow forecasts

Budgets

Budgeting lies at the foundation of every financial plan. It is about understanding how much money a business has, where it goes and how best to allocate those funds. A **budget** is a financial plan that estimates revenue and costs over a period of time.

Although each area within a business is likely to have its own budget, we normally distinguish between three types of budget:

- expenditure budget, which sets out the expected expenditure (costs) for a business over a given period of time
- revenue budget, which provides a projection of the future sales of the business
- profit budget, which combines both expenditure and revenue budgets to show expected profit

When constructing a budget it is important to use figures that are as accurate as possible. The starting point is a forecast for the expected sales and revenue. Once a business knows the expected sales, the likely expenditure can be estimated. Finally, revenue and expenditure can be put together to show the expected profit. The budget would normally be set out on a month-by-month basis, as shown in Figure 2 (p. 26).

Perhaps one of the most important aspects of budgeting lies in the analysis of the figures. This is normally undertaken in the form of **variance analysis**, where actual figures are compared to budgeted figures, as shown in Figure 3 (p. 26). Variance means the difference between the budgeted figures and the actual figures. The variances for the 5 months given in Figure 3 example are shown in Figure 4 (p. 26).

In the variance column there is a note to state whether the variance is favourable (F) or adverse (A). The variance is favourable if the actual profit is higher than the budget, for example if sales are greater than expected or costs less than expected. The variance is adverse if the actual profit is lower than expected, for example if sales were less or costs higher than budgeted.

Budget An estimation of the revenues and costs over a specified future time period.

Variance analysis The process of explaining the differences (variances) between budgeted figures and actual figures.

	January £ (000s)	February £ (000s)	March £ (000s)	April £ (000s)	May £ (000s)
Income					
Sales revenue	27.0	28.0	28.0	30.0	32.0
Expenditure					
Materials	15.0	15.5	15.5	16.0	16.5
Labour	8.0	8.0	8.0	8.0	8.0
Administration	1.0	1.0	1.0	1.0	1.0
Marketing	2.0	2.0	2.0	2.0	2.0
Total	26.0	26.5	26.5	27.0	27.5
Profit	**1.0**	**1.5**	**1.5**	**3.0**	**4.5**

Figure 2 A simple budget

	January £ (000s)		February £ (000s)		March £ (000s)		April £ (000s)		May £ (000s)	
	Budget	Actual	Budget	Actual	Budget	Actual	Budget	Actual	Budget	Actual
Income										
Sales revenue	27.0	27.0	28.0	27.5	28.0	27.5	30.0	28.0	32.0	29.0
Expenditure										
Materials	15.0	15.0	15.5	15.5	15.5	15.5	16.0	15.5	16.5	16.0
Labour	8.0	8.0	8.0	8.0	8.0	8.0	8.0	8.0	8.0	8.0
Administration	1.0	1.0	1.0	1.0	1.0	1.0	1.0	1.0	1.0	1.0
Marketing	2.0	2.0	2.0	2.0	2.0	2.0	2.0	2.5	2.0	2.5
Total	26.0	26.0	26.5	26.5	26.5	26.5	27.0	27.0	27.5	27.5
Profit	**1.0**	**1.0**	**1.5**	**1.0**	**1.5**	**1.0**	**3.0**	**1.0**	**4.5**	**1.5**

Figure 3 Comparing budgeted and actual figures

	Budget £ (000s)	Actual £ (000s)	Variance £ (000s)
Income			
Sales revenue	145.0	139.0	6.0 (A)
Expenditure			
Materials	78.5	77.5	1.0 (F)
Labour	40.0	40.0	0
Administration	5.0	5.0	0
Marketing	10.0	11.0	1.0 (A)
Total	133.5	133.5	0
Profit	11.5	5.5	6.0 (A)

Figure 4 Variance analysis

Knowledge check 20

What do you understand by the term 'variance analysis'?

Cash flow forecasts

A cash flow forecast is a prediction (forecast) of money coming into and flowing out of a business. At first sight this may seem similar to a budget but it is important to understand how they are different. The overall budget gives an indication of the likely profit at the end of the set time period, whereas the cash flow forecast shows the likely bank balance at the end of the set time period. In the cash flow forecast, inflows and outflows are recorded when they are likely to occur and therefore a business can easily see if it likely to run out of cash. A simple cash flow forecast is shown in Figure 5.

	January £ (000s)	February £ (000s)	March £ (000s)	April £ (000s)	May £ (000s)
Cash in					
Sales	10.0	11.0	11.5	12.0	12.5
Cash out					
Materials	7.0	7.5	7.5	8.0	8.0
Labour	1.0	1.0	1.0	1.0	1.0
Administration	0.5	0.5	0.5	0.5	0.5
Other costs	0	0	0	0.5	0
Total	8.5	9.0	9.0	10.0	9.5
Net cash flow	1.5	2.0	2.5	2.0	3.0
Opening balance	(5.5)	(4.0)	(2.0)	0.5	1.5
Closing balance	(4.0)	(2.0)	(0.5)	1.5	4.5

Figure 5 A cash flow forecast

The key points to note are:
- net cash flow is the difference between all cash in and all cash out
- opening balance is the amount carried forward from the previous month (that month's closing balance)
- closing balance is the sum of the net cash flow and opening balance

Cash flow forecasts are important as they can give an early indication of any cash shortages and enable corrective action to be taken. They are also important in support of loan applications as they will give a bank manager an indication of a business's ability to service monthly repayments.

The value of budgeting

Budgeting is important for a number of reasons:
- **Planning**. Budgets require managers to think about and plan what is happening in their business. The act of planning provides a financial roadmap for operations and can help to avoid unnecessary expenditure.
- **Assessing performance**. By analysing budgets and variances, it is possible to make an assessment of business performance.
- **Motivation**. Budgets can be motivating for the budget-holder.

How to construct and interpret break-even charts

A break-even chart is a graph used in break-even analysis to illustrate the output at which a business's total sales revenue is equal to its total costs and it neither makes a profit nor a loss (i.e. it breaks even). In order to construct a break-even chart it is necessary to understand the following terms:

- revenue — money received from the sales of a product or service
- fixed costs — costs that do not change with output, for example rent
- variable costs — costs that vary directly with output, for example materials
- total costs — fixed costs plus variable costs

The first stage in constructing a break-even chart is to establish the X (horizontal) and Y (vertical) axes. Output is plotted on the X axis and for this you will need to know the maximum output of the business. Costs and revenue are plotted on the Y axis. The extent of the axis is determined by the maximum amount of revenue achievable by the business.

Having established the axes, it is now possible to plot:

- **Total revenue.** Calculate the total revenue at maximum output (sales price per unit × output) and plot this on the chart. Then connect this point to the origin.
- **Fixed costs.** Fixed costs stay the same no matter what the output and what you will have on your chart is a horizontal line running parallel to the X axis at the level of fixed costs.
- **Variable costs.** Calculate the variable costs at maximum output (variable costs per unit × output). Plot this point on your chart and connect this point to the origin.
- **Total costs.** Add together the fixed costs and variable costs and plot this point on your chart. Then connect this point to the value of fixed costs on the Y axis.

These lines are shown in Figure 6.

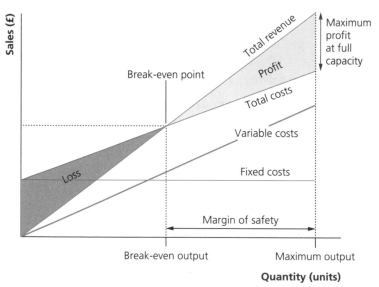

Figure 6 A break-even chart

How to calculate and illustrate on a break-even chart the effects of changes in price, output and cost

When drawing a break-even chart, it is always worth checking its accuracy by calculation. This can be done using the concept of **contribution**. This is the difference between revenue and variable costs and is calculated as follows:

Contribution = sales revenue − variable costs

It can also be calculated as contribution per unit as follows:

$$\text{Contribution per unit} = \frac{\text{sales revenue} - \text{variable costs}}{\text{output}}$$

Or, another way to calculate contribution per unit:

Contribution per unit = sales price per unit − variable costs per unit

It follows from this second calculation that total contribution can also be calculated by multiplying the unit contribution by output. Below the break-even point any contribution goes towards covering the fixed costs of production and above the break-even point any contribution is profit. Therefore, at the break-even output the value of total contribution is equal to the value of fixed costs. From this knowledge comes the formula for calculating the break-even output: divide fixed costs by the contribution per unit to arrive at the number of units that need to be produced to exactly cover the fixed costs:

$$\text{Break-even output} = \frac{\text{fixed costs}}{\text{contribution per unit}}$$

It is worth pointing out that contribution can also be used as an alternative way of calculating profit. Contribution is calculated by deducting variable costs from revenue, so if we take this further and deduct the fixed costs from the contribution total we will arrive at the profit figure as follows:

Profit = total contribution − fixed costs

Break-even charts can be a useful analytical tool for investigating the impact of changes in price and cost on break-even point and profit.

- **Impact on break-even point**. A rise in price leads to a lower break-even point, whereas a fall in price leads to a higher break-even point. A change in costs has the opposite effect: a rise in costs leads to a rise in break-even point, whereas a fall in costs leads to a fall in break-even point.
- **Impact on profit**. A rise in price leads to a rise in profit at any given output above break-even point and a fall in price leads to lower profit at any given output above break-even point. A rise in costs leads to lower profit and a fall results in greater profit at any given output above break-even point.

Another useful concept relating to break-even analysis is that of *margin of safety*. This is the difference between the actual output of a business and its break-even output:

Margin of safety = actual output − break-even output

This indicates the cushion or amount by which sales could fall before a business becomes loss-making.

Contribution The difference between sales revenue and variable costs.

Knowledge check 21

How is contribution used to calculate the following?
(a) Break-even output.
(b) Profit.

The value of break-even analysis

Break-even analysis is a simple and easy-to-use tool for managers, particularly for smaller businesses and those offering a single product. It can be useful in support of an application for a bank loan as it provides evidence of business planning and ability to **service a debt**. It can also be useful when analysing potential changes in price or costs and how such changes may affect profitability.

Break-even analysis, however, does have its limitations and these are associated with its simplicity. Not only does it assume that all products are sold, it also assumes that they are sold at the same price which in practice is unlikely on both counts. It also assumes costs remain the same, which again is unlikely. Fixed costs are likely to rise over time and variable costs might change, for example as a result of bulk buying. Finally, it becomes difficult to use break-even analysis when looking at a multi-product business.

How to analyse profitability

When looking at profit on p. 22, two ratios were identified:

$$\text{Gross profit margin} = \frac{\text{gross profit}}{\text{sales revenue}} \times 100$$

$$\text{Operating profit margin} = \frac{\text{operating profit}}{\text{sales revenue}} \times 100$$

We can add to a further equation, which is profit for the year margin:

$$\text{Profit for the year margin} = \frac{\text{profit for year}}{\text{sales revenue}} \times 100$$

Ratios are key to the analysis of financial performance — in this case, profitability. A figure for profit on its own tells the reader little other than whether it has risen or fallen. What the analyst really wants to know is whether there has been an overall improvement. This can only be shown when comparing figures for previous years or figures for other businesses, and this is achieved by examining profit margins. The percentage figure arrived at indicates how much of every pound of sales is profit. A 5% operating profit margin tells us that 5p of every pound sold is profit. This is a much more effective way of analysing a business's profitability and provides a meaningful judgement on performance.

How to analyse timings of cash inflows and outflows

The cash flow forecast is an important document that can be used to support loan applications as well as analysing the cash position of the business. This is usually in relation to the timings of inflows and outflows — if cash is slow in coming into the business but leaves it quickly, this can result in serious cash flow problems.

The money leaving the business is referred to as **payables** and the money coming into the business as **receivables**. It is important to investigate how quickly a business pays its *trade creditors* (those it owes money to for resources) and how long it takes to receive payments from its *trade debtors* (those who owe money to the business for goods and services received). These are measured in days and, if there is a big

Service a debt Refers to being able to make the repayments on any loans.

Knowledge check 22

Outline briefly the main problems associated with break-even analysis.

Exam tip

A profit figure on its own tells us little and in order to be useful it needs to be compared. This is most effectively done by the use of profit margins.

Payables Money owed to trade creditors by a business.

Receivables Money owed by trade debtors (customers) to a business.

difference between the number of days taken to pay and the number of days for receivables, this could indicate potential cash flow problems. The practice of allowing customers time to pay or not paying immediately for goods and services received is known as *trade credit*.

The use of data for financial decision-making and planning

Budgets, cash flow and break-even analysis provide managers with a huge amount of information and data. The analysis of this data, coupled with profitability data and analysis, provides the basis for financial decision-making. This makes for a more scientific approach and therefore helps reduce risk in decision-making. This is not only illustrated by the importance of cash flow forecasts in loan applications, it also involves every decision the business makes, such as launching a new product or investing in new production facilities. All of these factors have a financial implication that needs careful consideration and analysis of data in order to reduce risk.

Opportunities for analysis

- Analysis of the factors to consider when undertaking variance analysis.
- Analysis of the benefits of budgeting.
- Analysis of the benefits of financial data in decision-making.

Opportunities for evaluation

- The extent to which break-even analysis is a useful tool.
- Evaluation of the usefulness of budgets, cash flow forecasts and variance analysis in the decision-making process.

Making financial decisions: sources of finance

A business obtains its finance from a source. Finance may be raised internally or externally and be either short term or long term.

Internal and external sources of finance

Internally, the most important source of finance is **retained profit**, which is profit that is reinvested back into the business. Although shareholders who adopt a short-term approach might be upset at losing potential dividends, the hope is that using profit in this way creates growth in the long term. It also has a number of benefits over external sources of finance. Loans carry interest payments and eventually have to be paid back, whereas issuing further shares dilutes ownership. Using retained profit does, of course, require the firm to be profit-making in the first place.

Another source of internal finance is the sale of assets, which involves selling off an asset that is surplus to requirements. For example, it may be that a business has rationalised its activities and now operates out of one site instead of two, or alternatively the adoption of a just-in-time approach to production has created surplus warehousing space that can be sold off. Like retained profit, the sale of assets has the big advantage of no interest payments and no payback. Once sold, however, the assets are removed from the business so it needs to be sure it no longer has a need for them.

> **Knowledge check 23**
>
> Distinguish between trade creditors and trade debtors.

> **Retained profit** The profit that is kept within the business rather than paid out to shareholders as dividends.

Although these internal sources of finance may be used for short-term purposes, they are mainly long term in nature. On the other hand, external sources can be split into distinct short- or long-term sources.

Short-term finance includes overdrafts, debt factoring and trade credit. An *overdraft* is a short-term loan from a bank. *Debt factoring* involves passing debtors' invoices to a debt-factoring business for collection. Up to 80% of the value of the invoices is received immediately and the rest, less any costs, once the factoring company has collected them. *Trade credit* involves receiving materials now but paying for them at a later date.

In the long term, major sources of finance fall into two categories: *equity* and *borrowing*. Equity is share capital and borrowing involves loans from a bank. Also included here are *venture capital* and *debentures*. Venture capital is finance that is provided by venture capitalists for small- to medium-sized businesses and this source of finance is, by its nature, more risky. It may be in the form of loans or equity. A debenture is a specific type of loan.

Advantages and disadvantages of different sources of finance for short- and long-term uses

The advantages and disadvantages of internal sources of finance are covered above. External sources have the following benefits and drawbacks:

- Overdrafts are generally quick to arrange and the business benefits from paying interest only on the amount overdrawn and not the full amount of the overdraft. It therefore represents a flexible form of short-term finance.
- Debt factoring is useful when finance is required quickly and it does save a business the administrative expense of chasing its debtors. Its main disadvantage is that a percentage of the money owed by debtors goes to the debt-factoring company.
- Trade credit is useful as it is a means of delaying payment for materials and services, but as a result the business may lose out on certain prompt payment bonuses.
- Equity has the benefit of not having to be paid back and has no interest to be paid and dividends are given only to shareholders from profit. It does, however, result in dilution of share capital and for family businesses that turn public they may eventually lose their controlling interest.
- Borrowing can be quick to set up and avoids dilution of share capital, but it does have a number of drawbacks. It has to be paid back and incurs interest payments. As a result, servicing debt can become a problem, especially if interest rates are rising.

Opportunities for analysis

- Analysis of the benefits of internal sources of finance.
- Analysis of the benefits and drawbacks of external sources of finance.
- Analysis of the benefits of overdrafts.

Opportunities for evaluation

- The extent to which loans or equity might be the best source of finance.
- Evaluation of the various methods of short-term finance.

Exam tip

When analysing potential long-term sources of finance, an examination of a business's capital structure and capital gearing are likely to be key factors influencing the final decision made.

Knowledge check 24

Outline briefly the benefits of raising money through equity rather than borrowing.

Making financial decisions: improving cash flow and profits

Businesses are always looking for ways to improve cash flow and profits.

Methods of improving cash flow

There are a number of ways in which a business might improve its cash flow position:

- **Speed up inflows**. A business could try to speed up its inflows by perhaps being more rigorous in chasing late payments (better credit control) and debtors or by shortening the credit period allowed.
- **Slow down outflows**. A business might try to negotiate more favourable credit terms in order to slow down outflows.
- **Debt factoring**. By using the services of a debt-factoring agency, a business receives money sooner.
- **Short-term borrowing**. Many businesses use an overdraft facility in order to overcome a difficult cash flow position.

Methods of improving profits and profitability

There are a number of ways in which a business might improve profitability:

- **Reduce costs**. If costs can be reduced while maintaining the same selling price and sales level, profits will improve. This might be achieved by improvements in efficiency such as the introduction of new technology or the employment of lean production methods, as well as by moving production to a cheaper location or sourcing cheaper suppliers.
- **Increase prices**. If prices can be increased without a fall in demand, profits are likely to improve. This may be possible only for goods and services that are inelastic in nature.

Difficulties of improving cash flow and profit

In highly competitive markets and where suppliers also face financial pressures, improving cash flow and profits may be difficult in practice.

Attempts to improve cash flow can result in difficulties. Changing credit terms to customers or being more rigorous in chasing debtors can mean that relationships with customers are harmed: a slightly longer credit period is a USP and this may be the reason why customers come to them rather than a competitor. Relationships with suppliers might also be damaged by trying to extend the business's credit period, or changing to a cheaper supplier may affect flexibility and reliability. Debt factoring and overdrafts also come with costs that may worsen the situation in the long term.

Attempts to improve profits by the reduction of costs may lead to quality issues with a product or service, or perhaps ethical issues if goods are sourced from sweatshops overseas. If labour is reduced because of the introduction of new technology or redundancies occur because of relocating overseas, a business's reputation may be harmed. Raising prices is also likely to lead to criticism of putting shareholders before customers.

Knowledge check 25

Explain briefly why attempts to improve cash flow may lead to damaged relationships with customers and suppliers.

Content Guidance

Opportunities for analysis

- Analysis of the difficulties involved with improving cash flow or profits.

Opportunities for evaluation

- Evaluation of the various methods to improve cash flow or profits.

Summary

- Financial targets and the value of setting them.
- The distinction between cash flow and profit.
- The distinction between gross profit, operating profit and profit for the year and how to calculate margins.
- The setting of targets for revenue, costs, profit and cash flow.
- Capital structure and investment targets and the importance of capital gearing.
- External and internal influences on financial objectives and decisions.
- Break-even charts, their construction and interpretation.
- Contribution and the calculation of break-even output. The effects of changes in price output and costs on the break-even point and margin of safety.

- The value of break even, its benefits and drawbacks.
- The analysis and interpretation of profitability ratios: gross profit, operating profit and profit for the year margins.
- Analysis of cash flow timings, payables and receivables.
- The use of data in financial decision-making and planning.
- Internal and external sources of finance. The distinction between short- and long-term sources and the advantages and disadvantages of each.
- Methods of improving cash flow and profitability.

■ Decision-making to improve human resource performance

Human resources (HR) is the function of an organisation that is focused on activities of employees. These activities normally include recruitment, training, retention, motivation, welfare and benefits.

Setting human resource objectives

Human resource management involves matching the workforce to the business needs — having the right number of staff in the right place and with the correct skills. Human resource objectives focus on the recognition of human capital as a resource that drives business success.

The value of setting human resource objectives

The value of setting human resource objectives include:

- **Employee engagement**. Creating an environment where employees are enthusiastic about their job all the time — employees are motivated.
- **Compliance**. Aligning company policies with government and EU laws regarding health and safety and employment.
- **Turnover and retention**. Reducing turnover and increasing the retention of employees. In doing so, recruitment costs are reduced.
- **Employer of choice**. As an employer of choice, a company is the one all employees would be happy to be a part of.

As a result, a business might set the following objectives:

- **Employee engagement and involvement**. Having employees engaged and involved in a business leads to greater motivation and, as result, greater output and quality.
- **Talent development**. The recognition of potential within certain 'star' employees and the development and retention of those employees.
- **Training**. The improvement of workforce performance through the development of skills.
- **Diversity**. This concept encompasses acceptance and respect. It means understanding that each individual is unique and recognises individual differences. This can be along the lines of race, gender, age, sexual orientation, physical ability, religion, etc.
- **Alignment of values**. Bringing together employee values and business values.
- **Number skills and location of employees**. Over time, the nature of a business and production changes and it is crucial the human resources department ensures they always have the right employees in the right place with the correct skills.

Internal and external influences on human resource objectives and decisions

Like the other functional areas, objectives and decision-making within human resources are affected by a number of internal and external factors.

Internally, the overall corporate objectives and the resources available (especially finance) have an impact on objectives and decision-making. The type of product, whether it is a hi-tech innovative industry or one that simply assembles products on a production line, also has an impact. The style of management adopted is likely to have a big impact, whether a hard or soft approach is used:

- A hard approach to management is where employees are treated simply as a resource. With such an approach there is minimum communication and little empowerment and delegation. Appraisal systems focus on judgements about good or bad performance, and pay is at a minimum wage in order to recruit and retain staff.
- A soft approach to management involves regular communication with the workforce and employees are empowered and encouraged to take responsibility. Appraisal systems focus more on identifying and addressing employee needs, and pay structures are competitive and may encompass performance-related rewards such as profit-sharing.

Externally, PEST factors have a big impact on objectives and decisions:

- Politically — employment and health and safety laws are subject to regular refinement both from UK and European legislation, which the human resources department must keep abreast of.
- Economically — the stage of the economic cycle, together with changes in interest rates and exchange rates, has an ongoing effect on demand and therefore a business's requirement for labour resources. A business needs to be able to respond quickly and effectively to these changes.
- Socially — a business needs to recognise changes in attitudes and ensure its human resources policies are diverse and encompass all.
- Technologically — the environment is in a state of constant development and the human resources department needs to keep up to date, ensuring it has the right number of workers with the correct skills to embrace any developments.

As well as these factors, the human resources department also has to consider the wider market and competitive environment as changes here will have a big impact on workforce requirements, both positively and negatively.

Opportunities for analysis

- Analysis of the benefits of setting human resource objectives.
- Analysis of the internal and external factors affecting the setting and achievement of human resource objectives.

Opportunities for evaluation

- The extent to which internal and external factors might be more important influences on the achievement of human resource objectives.
- The extent to which one human resource objective (e.g. engagement) might be the most important objective.

Appraisal system The process by which a manager examines and evaluates an employee's work by comparing it with preset targets.

Knowledge check 26

Distinguish between a hard and a soft approach to human resource management.

Analysing human resource performance

Calculating and interpreting human resource data

As a means of analysing human resource data, there are a number of calculations that may be undertaken. These calculations relate to the effectiveness of the workforce, the cost of the workforce and its turnover and retention.

Labour productivity

Labour productivity measures the output per employee over a specified time period and is calculated using the following formula:

$$\text{Labour productivity} = \frac{\text{total output per time period}}{\text{number of employees}}$$

This is a key measure of business efficiency and is of particular importance as labour costs make up a significant proportion of a business's costs. The more units that can be produced per worker, the fewer workers that are needed. This may result in lower labour costs and increased competiveness.

However, productivity is likely to be affected by a number of factors. The amount of investment in technology (a more capital-intensive business) is likely to have greater productivity than a labour-intensive business. The skills and motivation of the workforce also have a big impact: a highly skilled and engaged workforce is likely to be more productive than a poorly skilled and engaged workforce. External factors such as the state of the economy also have an impact, such as a business adjusting to falling demand in a recession.

Labour cost per unit

This measures how much it costs in labour to produce one unit of output and is calculated as follows:

$$\text{Labour costs per unit} = \frac{\text{labour costs}}{\text{output}}$$

Labour costs per unit are related to productivity: if productivity rises, unit labour costs fall and if productivity falls, unit labour costs rise. Improving productivity may therefore be targeted in order to reduce labour costs per unit.

Employee costs as a percentage of turnover

As an alternative to unit labour costs it is also possible to calculate labour costs as a percentage of turnover. This is calculated as follows:

$$\text{Employee costs as a percentage of turnover} = \frac{\text{labour costs}}{\text{turnover}} \times 100$$

For many businesses, labour represents the biggest single cost. This is particularly true for premiership football clubs and some independent schools. Keeping labour costs within a sustainable percentage of turnover is therefore crucial to the survivability of these businesses.

Knowledge check 27

Outline briefly the factors that affect labour productivity.

Exam tip

A certain amount of labour turnover is inevitable and this level varies from industry to industry. It is therefore important to compare labour turnover and retention figures to the average for a particular industry in order to make a useful judgement.

Labour turnover and retention rates

These next two calculations measure how effective a business is in retaining its staff. They are calculated as follows:

$$\text{Labour turnover} = \frac{\text{number of employees leaving over the time period}}{\text{total number of employees}} \times 100$$

$$\text{Labour retention} = \frac{\text{number of employees employed for more than 1 year}}{\text{total number of employees}} \times 100$$

Although it is inevitable that some employees will leave over time because of **natural wastage**, the business will seek to avoid large and unnecessary labour turnover and, as far as possible, wishes to keep its most valuable and skilled staff. High levels of turnover and low levels of retention are likely to indicate an unhappy workforce.

The use of data for human resource decision-making and planning

Human resource planning is a key activity as it is essential that the business has the correct amount of labour with the correct skills. For example, rapid changes in technology have affected both the manufacturing and service sectors and human resources should plan effectively for these changes. Human resource managers need to be aware of current developments and gather information and data related to these as supporting evidence for future plans and skill development required.

Data on the business's existing workforce can be useful in developing plans. Trends may be spotted indicating potential problems ahead, for example if retention rates are slowly declining or labour turnover rates edging up. It may be possible to compare existing data with other firms or an industry average, which may help in identifying potential problems at an early stage. On its own, a slow improvement to the labour productivity figure may seem acceptable, but if competitors are showing a significant rise this could spell problems in the future that need to be addressed immediately.

Opportunities for analysis

- Analysis of the benefits and drawbacks of human resource data.

Opportunities for evaluation

- Evaluation of the usefulness of human resource data.

Making human resource decisions: improving organisational design and managing human resource flow

Organisational structure is the formal framework of policies and rules within which an organisation arranges its lines of authority and communication and allocates rights and duties. It determines the manner in which roles, power and responsibilities are delegated, controlled and coordinated and how information flows between levels of management. Organisational design is a process that is likely to change and evolve over time in order to enable an organisation to operate more efficiently, learn faster and change more easily.

Natural wastage The reduction in size of a workforce through voluntary resignation or retirement rather than redundancy.

Human resource planning The process that links the human resource needs of an organisation to its strategic plan to ensure staffing is sufficient, qualified and competent enough to achieve organisational objectives.

Knowledge check 28

Distinguish between labour turnover and labour retention.

The **human resource flow** refers to the flow of workers through an organisation and was first coined by Michael Beer in 1984. Beer recognised people as the main asset of an organisation and therefore how employee influence plays a major role. In order to have fully engaged workers, the human resource flow needs to be carefully managed, from recruiting, transfer and promotion and, finally, through to termination of employment. The organisation must meet employee requirements in terms of reward systems and work systems in order to achieve full commitment and engagement to the organisational needs.

Knowledge check 29

Why is it important to have fully engaged employees?

Influences on job design

Job design is the process of deciding on the contents of a job in terms of its duties and responsibilities, on the methods to be used to carry out the job and on the relationships that should exist between the job holder and their superiors. A well-designed job is likely to make the job more interesting and lead to increased performance and engagement of the workforce. In order to achieve greater engagement, a number of ideas have been put forward related to job design.

Job rotation

Rather than simply having one set task, employees may be asked to rotate round a number of tasks. Although this provides variety and may relieve the monotony of undertaking only one task, it requires the employee to learn more tasks without necessarily any greater reward.

Job enlargement

This is similar to job rotation, but instead of rotating round different jobs the role itself is increased to include more tasks. Often referred to as 'horizontal loading' as the tasks are all at the same level, it suffers from the same disadvantages as job rotation.

Job enrichment

This differs from job enlargement in that it is vertically loaded — it is not only about increasing the number of tasks but also their complexity. Employees are given more responsibility for managing themselves and problem-solving. As a result, jobs should be more satisfying and lead to greater engagement and commitment.

Empowerment

This is related to job enrichment and is a term used today to describe the process of redesigning a job to give workers greater control over their working lives. The concepts of enrichment and **empowerment** are taken further in the Hackman and Oldham theory, as shown in Figure 7 on p. 40.

This model is based on the idea that the task itself is key to employee motivation. A boring, monotonous job stifles motivation, whereas a challenging job enriches motivation. Variety, autonomy and decision-making are three ways of adding challenge to a job. It states there are five core job dimensions (skill variety, task identity, task significance, autonomy and feedback) that impact on three critical psychological states (experienced meaningfulness of the work, experienced responsibility for outcomes of the work and knowledge of the actual results), which in turn influence personal and work outcomes (work motivation, work performance, work satisfaction

Empowerment The concept in management that if employees are given the right information and resources and a degree of control over their work, they are likely to be more productive.

and low absenteeism). The five core job dimensions can be combined to form a motivating potential score for a job that can be used as an index of how likely a role is to affect attitudes and behaviour.

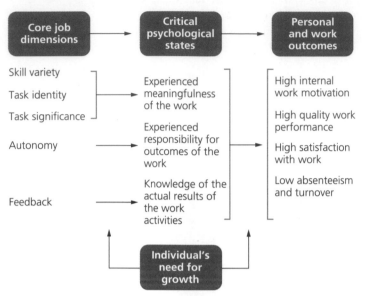

Figure 7 The Hackman and Oldham job characteristics model

The model suggests high motivation is related to experiencing the three critical psychological states while working. In turn, each of these three states is derived from certain characteristics of the job. From knowing these critical job characteristics, so the theory goes it is then possible to derive the key components of the design of the job and redesign it.

Knowledge check 30

Outline briefly the Hackman and Oldham model.

Influences on job design can be categorised into three main groups:

■ **Organisational factors** such as the nature of the work and the culture of the business, which determine the extent and willingness of an organisation to design jobs in such a way that enrichment and empowerment exist.
■ **Behavioural factors** and the extent to which a job or task offers autonomy, diversity and the use of skills.
■ **Environmental factors** such as the availability of employees and their abilities as well as their socio-economic expectations.

Influences on organisational design

Organisational design is the process of constructing and adjusting an organisation's structure to achieve its goals. The organisational structure defines how tasks are divided, grouped and coordinated in an organisation. This is sometimes shown in an organisation chart that demonstrates the hierarchy of the business, with a **chain of command** that provides a line of authority from the top of the organisation to the bottom and shows who reports to whom.

The structure of the organisation also determines and depicts the *span of control*. This is the number of subordinates an individual manager can efficiently and effectively

Chain of command
The order in which authority and power in an organisation is wielded and delegated from top management to every employee at every level. Authority flows down the chain of command, whereas accountability flows up.

control. Organisations with wider spans of control require fewer managers and have a flatter structure, as shown in Figure 8a, whereas those with narrower spans are likely to have more managers and taller structures (Figure 8b). Flatter structures with wider spans tend to become more predominant as this gives greater scope for worker empowerment lower down the hierarchy.

(a)   **(b)**

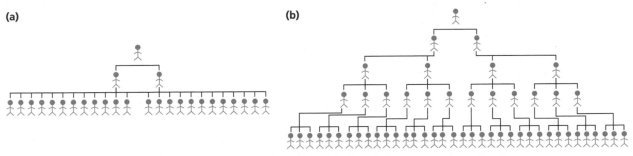

Figure 8 (a) A flat hierarchy/wider span of control; **(b)** A tall hierarchy/narrower span of control

An important element of an organisational structure is delegation. This relates to how authority passes through the organisation and it is a vital process. In a large organisation, it is impossible for one manager to take all the decisions. Therefore, delegation relieves them of the more routine decisions and allows them to concentrate on important strategic areas. Effective leaders use delegation to balance workloads and provide staff development opportunities. As a result, good delegation can create a positive motivating and engaging environment for employees.

Another aspect of organisational structure is centralisation and decentralisation, which determine where decision-making and authority lie. If top management make all the organisational decisions with no input from lower-level personnel, the organisation is centralised. The more lower-level personnel are involved, the greater the degree of decentralisation.

The following factors also influence organisational design:

- **Size**. It goes without saying that the larger the organisation, the more complex it is likely to be. As an organisation grows, it becomes increasingly difficult to manage and needs a formal structure. The structure that develops is one that allows it to operate effectively.
- **Life cycle**. Organisations go through a life cycle and it is likely the structure of the organisation will evolve with that life cycle.
- **Strategy**. The overall corporate objectives and resulting strategy determine the structure of an organisation. A company that wants to be innovative and ahead of the rest requires a different structure to one that simply wants to operate in a mass market.
- **Environment**. This dictates whether the organisation is operating in a stable environment, where customer desires are understood and remain consistent, or in a dynamic environment, where customer needs are changing constantly.
- **Technology**. This is used in almost all industries but the extent to which it is or can be used may to some extent help determine an organisation's structure.

Knowledge check 31

What do you understand by the terms 'hierarchy', 'span of control' and 'delegation'?

Influences on delegation, centralisation and decentralisation

A number of factors affect the extent of delegation, centralisation and decentralisation:

- **Uniformity of policy**. Uniformity of an organisation's policy determines the extent to which decentralisation can take place. If an organisation has uniform policies, these must be kept consistent and there will be little scope for decentralisation.
- **Size of the business**. Larger businesses tend to be far more complex and therefore provide greater scope for decentralisation.
- **Philosophy of the management**. This relates to the leadership style adopted by top management. An autocratic approach tends toward a centralised structure, whereas a more democratic approach leans more toward a decentralised structure.
- **Skills of the workforce**. A decentralised approach requires the workers to have relevant skills and, if these skills are not apparent, a more centralised approach is likely to be adopted.

It is also possible for external factors such as economic factors to have an influence. For example, during a recession there might be a greater pressure for a more centralised approach as organisations seek to cut back. What is happening in the market in which the firm operates and competitor actions may also have an influence. In terms of technology, the greater amount of data available to an organisation enables a greater degree of decentralisation. For example, in the retail industry having specific data related to individual stores allows a greater degree of individual control over what products to stock and when.

The value of changing job and organisational design

An organisation would not consider changing job or organisational design unless it expected potential benefits from doing so. In other words, some form of competitive advantage would be expected. This might come in the form of lower costs. For example, as a result of introducing a flatter structure (**delayering**), the cost of the managerial positions no longer in existence would be saved. Making jobs more interesting and rewarding may create a more engaged and motivated workforce, leading to higher productivity and better quality and resulting in lower unit labour costs. In summary, the value of such changes should come in helping a business to achieve its human resource objectives.

How managing human resource flow helps meet human resource objectives

Human resource flow is the movement of people through a business, starting with recruitment. However, before recruitment can take place it is necessary to have undertaken some form of human resource planning. This is the process that identifies the competencies a business needs to fulfil its goals and is shaped by organisational strategy. Its aim is to have the right number of people in the right place, with the right skills, at the right time, in order to fulfil its organisational objectives.

> **Knowledge check 32**
>
> Outline how the style of management and uniformity of policy influence the extent of centralisation and decentralisation.

> **Delayering** The process of cutting layers of management from an organisational hierarchy.

Recruitment and selection

The first stages in the recruitment and selection process are the drawing up of a **job description** and **person specification**. These outline the role and duties to be performed and the skills and attributes required to fill the job. Once this has been done, the organisation has to decide whether to recruit internally from within the business or externally. If externally, advertisements need to be placed, applications invited, shortlists drawn up and interviews undertaken before a final appointment is made.

Internal recruitment is cheaper than external recruitment and it benefits from the recruit already being familiar with the organisation. On the other hand, by recruiting externally it may be possible to acquire the specific skills needed and this is likely to bring new ideas into the business.

Training

This is an important part of the human resource flow that involves employees acquiring and developing their skills and is strongly associated with talent development. It might be undertaken either on the job, learning from present employees, or off the job on specific work-related courses at training centres, colleges and university. Training can improve efficiency and quality within a business as well as motivation of the workforce. However, training does not come cheap and, once trained, it is important to retain employees otherwise this money is wasted.

Dismissal

The final stage in the human resource flow is dismissal of an employee or termination of employment. Dismissal occurs only in specific circumstances:

- Gross misconduct — this may be because of theft or violence toward a customer or colleague.
- Persistent minor misconduct — if, after regular warnings (verbal and written), an employee persists in an offence such as regularly turning up late for work they may be dismissed.
- A substantial reason — this could be not agreeing to reasonable changes in employment terms.
- Redundancy — an employee is made redundant if their job no longer exists. This might be as a result of production moving elsewhere, the business closing or technology replacing labour. If those made redundant have been employed for two or more years, they are entitled to compensation. Redundancy may take place on a voluntary basis and an organisation must consult with individual employees as well as worker representatives if 20 or more people are made redundant at the same time. As an alternative to redundancy, workers may be offered redeployment (alternative employment) within the business. However, this may not be popular if such an offer means moving to a different location or the terms and conditions are vastly different to the existing contract.

Employment may be terminated by the employee, perhaps because of retirement, promotion or family reasons. Such termination is known as natural wastage and occurs in all organisations. Employees may also leave because they are unhappy in their job and, if this is the case, it is more worrying for the organisation and should be investigated. This emphasises the importance of analysing labour retention and turnover figures. (See p. 38 for more information on retention and labour turnover.)

Job description A broad written statement of a specific job based on the findings of job analysis. It generally includes the duties, purpose, responsibilities, scope and working conditions of a job.

Person specification A statement of the knowledge, skills, education and experience required of an applicant for a particular job.

Exam tip

Human resource flow is a term new to this specification, so it is important to make sure you understand what it means.

Having the right people in the right place, with the right skills, at the right time, in the right number and being able to retain them means a more engaged, committed and motivated workforce that is likely lead to the achievement of the human resource objectives.

Knowledge check 33

What are the main areas covered by the human resource flow?

Opportunities for analysis

- Analysis of the benefits and drawbacks of changing organisation or job design
- Analysis of the benefits and drawbacks of delegation.
- Analysis of the circumstances where decentralisation or centralisation might be most appropriate.
- Analysis of the benefits of managing the human resource flow.

Opportunities for evaluation

- Evaluation of the usefulness of the Hackman and Oldham model.
- The extent to which changing organisational or job design might enable a business to achieve its objectives.
- The extent to which human resource planning is crucial to the success of the business.

Making human resource decisions: improving motivation and engagement

The benefits of motivated and engaged employees

Employee engagement is the state of emotional and intellectual commitment to an organisation — the degree to which an organisation has captured the hearts and minds of its employees. Employee engagement and motivation are interlinked. If workers are not engaged with what they do or the people they work with, ultimately they are not committed to the success of the company. If employees are engaged and motivated, it could lead to the following benefits for the business:

- improved employee performance
- increased consumer satisfaction
- decreased labour turnover and greater retention of employees
- greater financial success

Engaged employees are likely to say consistently positive things about the organisation, stay with the organisation and strive to achieve above and beyond what is expected in their daily role (Figure 9).

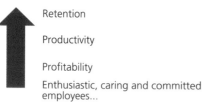

Retention

Productivity

Profitability

Enthusiastic, caring and committed employees...

Figure 9 The benefits of engaged employees

How to improve employee engagement and motivation

Perhaps the first step in improving engagement in an individual organisation is to identify the cause of any problems. Once this has been done, if any efforts to improve employee engagement are to be successful they need to be tailored to the needs of the individual. The following ideas may help toward this.

Leadership

Leaders need to show a genuine interest in their employees and understand their needs and aspirations. They need to show employees they are valued by listening to their suggestions and creating a rewarding environment in which to work.

Nature of the work

This needs to be meaningful and employees should believe that they are undertaking an important and valuable job. The connection between individual roles and the success of the business need to be apparent. Setting goals may also give a sense of purpose and if workers have a degree of autonomy over the way work is done and involvement in decision-making this is likely to make work all the more meaningful.

Recognition

Workers like to be recognised for their effort and praised for a job well done. Managers who recognise when they have gone the 'extra mile' are likely to encourage them and boost their performance. Such praise may elevate a worker's status within a business. In addition, competitive pay rates, benefits and overall working conditions also need to be good.

Opportunity

Many employees look for opportunities to demonstrate their skills and progress in a business. In this context, training and career development are important issues.

Culture

The culture of the business may also be important in establishing an engaged workforce. A people-focused culture that promotes the idea that employees are listened to and valued is perhaps more likely to have an engaged workforce.

Knowledge check 34

How might the nature of the job lead to a more engaged workforce?

The value of theories of motivation

Motivation of employees has been the subject of many articles and books with numerous theories put forward. The AQA specification identifies three writers in particular: Taylor, Maslow and Herzberg. These writers can be split into two groups: the scientific school of thought and the human relations school of thought.

Scientific school of thought

Frederick Winslow Taylor is perhaps the most important writer in this area. His theories on motivation are based on the belief that employees are motivated only by money. He saw employees as cogs in a machine rather than human beings. Therefore, anything that could be done to make that machine work better — that is, produce more and therefore potentially lead to more pay for employees — should be embraced by employees. As a result, Taylor undertook work study to improve the way the work was done (efficiency). He looked at tools and equipment and modified them to suit individual jobs. Training was also undertaken and piece rate pay used. This theory is based on completing the job more efficiently and is well documented in Taylor's writings related to Bethlehem Steel.

Human relations school of thought

This school of thought was brought to the fore by Elton Mayo. The key weakness of the scientific school was that it ignored the needs of the individual. Although Mayo himself was a follower of the scientific school his research threw up some interesting observations, the most notable of which were his studies at the Hawthorne Works in Chicago. The conclusions he drew from this were that:

- individual workers cannot be treated in isolation but must be seen as members of a group
- monetary incentives may be less important than belonging to a group
- managers must be aware of and cater for the social needs of employees

Later writers in the human relations school have often been referred to as the neo-human relations school and into this group come Abraham Maslow and Frederick Herzberg.

Maslow's hierarchy of needs

According to Maslow, workers have five types of needs and these form a hierarchy, as shown in Figure 10.

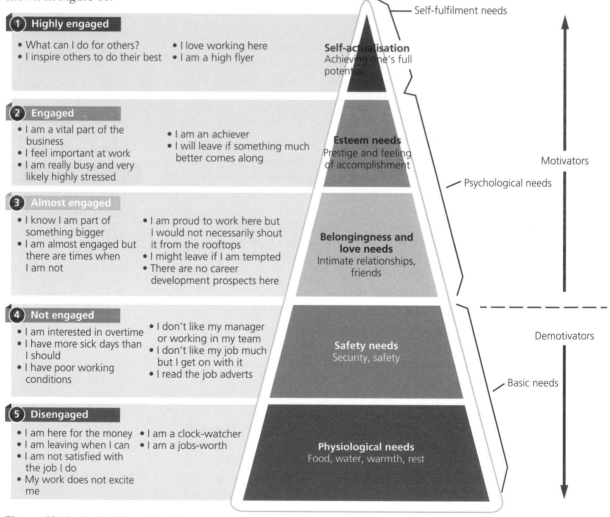

Figure 10 Maslow's hierarchy of needs

In terms of employee engagement and motivation, this hierarchy comprises:

- physiological needs — working conditions, pay, holidays etc.
- safety needs — security needs such as a safe working environment
- belongingness and love needs — team-working and contact with other employees
- esteem needs — achievement and recognition, chances for promotion
- self-actualisation — having challenging tasks that enable someone to reach their full potential

Using Maslow's hierarchy, it can be seen that simply providing good working conditions and a secure environment to work in will not on their own create an engaged workforce. In order to become engaged, it is necessary to satisfy the esteem and self-actualisation needs. This idea is further supported by Herzberg's two-factor theory.

Herzberg's motivation–hygiene theory

Herzberg divided the factors that motivate people into two groups:

- **Motivating factors**. Herzberg claimed certain factors lead to motivation, such as giving responsibility, recognition and the chance for advancement.
- **Hygiene factors**. These on their own may not create motivation. However, Herzberg suggested that they are necessary for workers to be motivated as they remove dissatisfaction. They include things such as pay, job security and working conditions.

The theories outlined above each provide a slightly different approach to the motivation of employees, but what value do they have for management?

- **Taylor**. Although he ignored employees' social needs and assumed they were motivated only by money, his work does have some value. He established the management of business as a subject for study and the ideas of work study and piece rate are still used today.
- **Mayo**. Perhaps his greatest contribution is in the importance of group- or team-working.
- **Maslow and Herzberg**. Although different, there are some similarities in the work of these two theorists and this is perhaps where their value lies. The higher esteem and self-actualisation needs of Maslow link clearly to the motivators of Herzberg. As we have seen earlier when referring to worker engagement, recognition, responsibility, status and involvement in decision-making are essential to motivation.

The use of financial methods of motivation

Workers can be motivated by different methods of payment:

- **Piece rate**. This is where workers are paid by each item they produce. This encourages them to work fast and produce more, but levels of quality could suffer and workers might require high levels of supervision as a result.
- **Commission**. Similar to piece rate but linked to sales, an employee is rewarded according to sales achieved.
- **Wages and salaries**. Wages are paid on an hourly rate and should be at or above the minimum wage. Any worker undertaking extra hours is paid overtime, often at

Knowledge check 35

Distinguish between the scientific and human relations schools of thought.

a higher hourly rate. Salaries are paid at an annual rate and divided into 12 equal instalments. There is no extra pay for working additional hours.

■ **Performance-related pay**. This is a method of payment linked to performance and usually measured against pre-agreed targets. Such a method may well be linked to an appraisal system.

Other financial methods that might be used include bonuses (such as profit-sharing), fringe benefits (such as company cars) and health insurance, as well share-ownership schemes.

The use of non-financial methods of motivating employees

Non-financial methods of motivation can be linked to the ideas of Maslow and Herzberg in that they often try to give greater responsibility, recognition and involvement to the workforce. We have already looked at the importance of job design and the concepts of job enrichment and empowerment (p. 39). The importance of good communication and training have also been discussed on p. 36. All these areas can be seen as non-financial methods of motivation. Added to the above should be that of team- or group-working in the form of autonomous work groups and quality circles.

Influences on the choice and assessment of the effectiveness of financial and non-financial reward systems

There are a number of factors that might affect the choice and effectiveness of a reward system:

■ **Cost**. A business must operate within its means and wants to keep a careful check on both unit labour costs and labour costs as a percentage of turnover.
■ **Type of work**. It is not only the type of work that has an influence, it is also the skills of the workforce involved. Reward and conditions of work need to be appropriate to attract and retain employees. If a business gets this right, it may well be able to establish a reputation as a good employer to work for.
■ **Culture**. The culture of the business is likely to have an influence on the type of management system used, for example whether it has a hard or soft approach to human resources.
■ **External factors**. These include the economic cycle — it may be difficult to have performance-related pay systems in times of economic recession.

Opportunities for analysis

■ Analysis of the factors affecting employee engagement.
■ Analysis of the benefits and drawbacks of motivation theories.
■ Analysis of the benefits and drawbacks of non-financial and financial methods of motivation.

Quality circles A group of workers who meet regularly to identify, analyse and solve work-related problems.

Knowledge check 36

Using examples, distinguish between financial and non-financial methods of motivation.

Opportunities for evaluation

- Evaluation of the usefulness of motivation theories to a particular business.
- The extent to which financial and non-financial methods of motivation are most appropriate to a particular business.
- The extent to which employee engagement is the most important factor in achieving a business's objectives.

Making human resource decisions: improving employer–employee relations

Influences on the extent and methods of employee involvement in decision-making

Good employer–employee relations are essential to the efficient running of a business. The extent of employee involvement in decision-making, however, is likely to depend on a number of factors:

- The management style and approach to human resource management — whether a hard (more autocratic) or soft (more democratic) approach is adopted. A hard approach is likely to have minimal involvement, whereas a soft approach may encourage involvement.
- The nature of the work and skill set of employees may well have an impact. Employees who are highly skilled and working in technical industries are likely to have more involvement in decision-making than those working on a production line.
- Legislation may also impact on employee involvement in decision-making, such as legislation relating to works councils and trade unions.

There is no common structure for employee representation and participation in the workplace and the extent of participation varies from organisation to organisation. As an individual's views usually carry little weight, employees are often represented collectively, either in the form of a trade union or works council.

Trade unions

Trade unions are organisations that represent the interests of employees in order to protect and advance their position in the workplace. Their role includes to:

- negotiate with employers on pay and conditions
- discuss major changes in the workplace such as redundancy
- accompany members in disciplinary and grievance meetings
- discuss members' concerns with employers
- provide members with legal and financial advice

The major benefit of membership of a trade union lies in the collective representation of the workforce when negotiating over pay and conditions and in the past this has often shown trade unions in a bad light. Despite this, trade unions undertake a great deal of good work relating to the other points above and this should not be overlooked.

Exam tip

Trade unions are often seen in a bad light, but they actually undertake a great deal of good work and this should not be overlooked. Improvements made in worker safety and conditions of work have, in part, come about as a result of trade union pressure.

Knowledge check 37

Outline briefly the role of trade unions.

Works councils

Works councils are a body composed of both employee and employer representatives elected to negotiate with management about working conditions, wages, etc. As their members are usually elected and include both employer and employee representatives, works councils may provide better communication and increased employee involvement, resulting in a more conciliatory relationship than that of a trade union.

How to manage and improve employer–employee communications and relations

Strong employer–employee relationships often lead to greater employee happiness, retention and significantly improved productivity. This relationship does not just happen; it needs to be worked on and managed effectively.

Key to this is perhaps communication that is open, honest and facilitates contribution from all. This requires a certain style of management and the necessary structures to be in place. This may, for example, involve a soft approach to management and empowerment of the workforce.

Sometimes disputes arise between employers and employees and when this happens it is important that they are resolved quickly. If this cannot be achieved within the business, the services of the **Advisory, Conciliation and Arbitration Service (ACAS)** may be employed. Conciliation is when a third party encourages both parties to come together and continue discussions. Arbitration is when a third party makes a judgement on a dispute and puts forward a settlement. This may be binding or non-binding.

Value of good employer–employee relations

A happy workforce is more likely to be a productive workforce and good employer–employee relations contribute to that happy workforce. The benefits of a good relationship are:

- Objectives — an organisation is more likely to meet both its human resources and corporate objectives with a happy, engaged and well-motivated workforce.
- Motivation — good employer–employee relations should lead to a well-motivated workforce, resulting in higher productivity and quality.
- Decision-making — it is likely decision-making will be more balanced by taking all views into consideration.
- Change — where good employer–employee relations exist, it is likely that change will be easier to implement as all perspectives are involved and taken into consideration.

Opportunities for analysis

- Analysis of the benefits and drawbacks of trade unions to a particular business.
- Analysis of the benefits of good employer–employee relations.

Opportunities for evaluation

- The extent to which good communication is the key to effective employer–employee relations.
- Evaluation of the factors affecting employer–employee relations.

Advisory, Conciliation and Arbitration Service (ACAS) A government organisation that provides information, advice, training and conciliation for employers and employees to help prevent or resolve workplace problems.

Knowledge check 38

Outline briefly the main benefit of good employer–employee relations.

Summary

- Human resource objectives, employee engagement, talent development, training, diversity, employee involvement, alignment of values and the skills and location of employees.
- Internal and external influences on management objectives. Internal influences include the hard or soft approach to management.
- Human resource data including the calculation of labour turnover and retention rates, labour productivity, labour cost per unit and labour costs as a percentage of turnover.
- The use of data in human resource planning.
- Influences on job design such as job enlargement, enrichment and empowerment, and how these are linked to the Hackman Oldham model.
- Organisational design and its impact on authority, span of control, hierarchy, delegation and centralisation and decentralisation.
- Influences on organisational design, size, life cycle of the business, strategy, environment and technology.
- Influences on centralisation/decentralisation and delegation including size of the business, nature and uniformity of the work, philosophy of the management and skills and abilities of the workforce.

- The value of changing organisational design in terms of motivation and engagement of the workforce.
- Human resource planning and human resource flow from recruitment, training and talent development to redeployment, redundancy and dismissal.
- The benefits of a motivated and engaged workforce and how to improve it.
- Theories of motivation and their value, such as the scientific school of Taylor, the human relations school of Mayo and the neo-human relations of Maslow and Herzberg.
- Financial and non-financial methods of motivation and the influences such as cost, nature of the work culture and external factors that affect their choice.
- Factors affecting employer–employee relations including style of management, nature of the work and the means by which relations are facilitated such as trade unions and works councils.
- Managing and improving relations through good communication and involvement and ACAS.
- The value of good employer–employee relations in terms of motivation and engagement.

Questions & Answers

This section contains a variety of exam-style questions that you are likely to encounter. The multiple-choice and short-answer questions are based on the content of this Student Guide; the data-response questions are directed at a specific area of content (operations management, finance and human resources); and the synoptic AS case study covers the content of both Student Guides 1 and 2. Note that essay questions are found only on A-level papers.

The correct answers for the multiple-choice questions are provided, together with commentary on why each answer is correct. For each short-answer, data-response, case study and essay question you will find sample answers with exam comments. One of the sample answers will be a good response and the other a weaker answer, with the aim of illustrating common errors made by students and examples of good practice in the hope that you will, with practice, be able to develop your own skills. For the quantitative skills questions practice, only the correct answers are given.

Questions

As the multiple-choice and short-answer questions give a broad coverage of the content of this book, it would make sense to use these towards the end of your revision period in order to check your knowledge. However, the data-response questions could be used as you complete an area of content.

Sample answers

Resist the temptation to study the answers before you have attempted the questions. If you make a mistake here it is not the end of the world and practice at developing your own responses will help you to hone your skills. Once you have written your answer, look at the sample responses and identify the strengths and weaknesses of your own work. Using the Questions & Answers section in this way should result in the quality of your answers improving.

Assessment

AS and A-level papers do not just test how well you know the content of the subject. There is a clear set of skills that are tested and it is essential that you are aware of these and have some idea of how to satisfy them. The following skills are tested:

- **Knowledge and understanding**. This relates to the content of the specification and how well you know and understand the various business concepts, theories and ideas.
- **Application**. This focuses on your ability to relate your knowledge and understanding of the subject content to a particular situation or scenario (such as that in a particular case study).
- **Analysis**. This is the ability to develop an extended line of argument related to a particular question.
- **Evaluation**. This is making a judgement by weighing up the evidence provided.

It is important to understand that not all questions test all the skills set out above and as a result it is important that you are able to recognise which skills are being tested. The basis of all questions will be some element of knowledge, but what other skills will be required? The clue to this is in the question command words. Some commonly used ones are outlined below.

Application

The following command words require you to apply your answer to the context of the question or case:

- 'Explain...'
- 'Calculate...'

Analysis

The following command words require you to develop a relevant argument:

- 'Analyse...'
- 'Explain why...'
- 'Examine...'

Remember that your answer has to be in context (application).

Evaluation

The following command words require you to make a judgement:

- 'Evaluate...'
- 'Discuss...'
- 'To what extent...'
- 'Justify...'

Remember again that in an answer that requires evaluation your arguments must be developed (analysis) and they must also be in context (application).

It is worth remembering that most students who have studied Business seriously and who under-perform do not do so because of a lack of knowledge but because of a lack of good exam technique. If you understand the skills that are being tested, recognise how to develop them and are prepared to practise them, you will be one step ahead of the game.

Multiple-choice questions (AS and A-level)

Question 1

Which of the following is not an operational objective? (1 mark)

A Dependability

B Flexibility

C Quality

D Labour retention

Question 2

What is the correct meaning of unit cost? (1 mark)

A The price of selling one unit

B The cost of selling one unit

C The cost of producing one unit

D Sales revenue divided by units produced

Question 3

Excess capacity in a business refers to: (1 mark)

A The extra capacity it is using

B The percentage of capacity it is not using

C The percentage of capacity it is using

D The amount of extra capacity it needs

Question 4

One advantage of a just-in-time stock control system is: (1 mark)

A It reduces the need for a business to plan its stock

B The business becomes more reliant on its suppliers

C It reduces the cost of holding stock

D It reduces the cost of stock

Question 5

In terms of stock control, lead time is: (1 mark)

A The time between ordering stock and its arrival

B The time between receiving stock and using it

C The time taken to use stock

D The time taken to order stock

Question 6

The capital gearing of a business refers to: (1 mark)

A   The amount of capital invested in a business

B   The relationship between borrowing and equity

C   The relationship between short- and long-term capital

D   How capital has been used in a business

Question 7

Company X Ltd achieved annual sales of £10.5m in 2014 and its direct costs of production were £6m. Which of the following represents its gross profit margin? (1 mark)

A   £4.5m

B   0.428%

C   4.5%

D   42.85%

Question 8

Which of the following is true at the break-even output? (1 mark)

A   Total costs = total profit

B   Total revenue = total profit

C   Fixed costs = total profit

D   Fixed costs = total contribution

Question 9

Which of the following represents an external source of long-term finance? (1 mark)

A   An overdraft

B   Retained profit

C   A bank loan

D   Sale of assets

Question 10

Which of the following is a method of improving cash flow? (1 mark)

A   Speeding up payments to trade creditors

B   Debt factoring

C   Increasing sales

D   Offering customers longer periods of trade credit

Question 11

Which of the following is least likely to be a characteristic of a soft approach to human relations? (1 mark)

A Employee involvement in decision-making

B Empowerment of the workforce

C An autocratic style of management

D Job enrichment

Question 12

What is the process by which a business determines how it should move from its current manpower position to its desired manpower position? (1 mark)

A Human resource management

B Recruitment

C Performance appraisal

D Human resource planning

Question 13

The process by which the aptitudes, skills and abilities of an employee are improved is known as: (1 mark)

A Training

B Performance appraisal

C Motivation

D Orientation

Question 14

According to Herzberg's motivation–hygiene theory, which of the following would not be considered to be a motivating factor? (1 mark)

A Good working conditions

B Responsibility

C Recognition

D Involvement in decision-making

Question 15

Which of the following is not a means of financial motivation? (1 mark)

A Performance-related pay

B Commission

C Autonomous work groups

D Piece rate

Answers to multiple-choice questions

Question 1

Correct answer D. (1 mark)

ⓔ Don't be too hasty when answering this question — read it carefully first. The question is which option is *not* an operational objective. Option D is a human resource objective.

Question 2

Correct answer C. (1 mark)

ⓔ It is the unit *cost* of production that is required in this question — quite easy, but make sure you read the options carefully.

Question 3

Correct answer B. (1 mark)

ⓔ 'Excess capacity' means the extra capacity that the business is not currently using.

Question 4

Correct answer C. (1 mark)

ⓔ An advantage of just-in-time production is required here, so the correct answer is that it reduces the cost of holding stock as less stock is held with the system.

Question 5

Correct answer A. (1 mark)

ⓔ This should be a relatively straightforward question — lead time is the time between ordering stock and its arrival.

Question 6

Correct answer B. (1 mark)

ⓔ Capital gearing refers to the percentage of total capital that is borrowing and therefore analyses the relationship between borrowing and equity.

Question 7

Correct answer D. (1 mark)

ⓔ If you know the formula, this is an easy calculation. When calculating, make sure you work it as a percentage and that you have the decimal point in the right place.

Question 8

Correct answer D.
(1 mark)

e This question is just a matter of knowledge and remembering that fixed costs = total contribution at the break-even output.

Question 9

Correct answer C.
(1 mark)

e An external and long-term source is required, so the correct answer is a bank loan.

Question 10

Correct answer B.
(1 mark)

e Improving cash flow can be achieved by speeding up inflows or slowing down outflows and the only option that achieves this is debt factoring.

Question 11

Correct answer C.
(1 mark)

e Read the question carefully — it asks which option is the *least* likely to be a characteristic of a soft approach.

Question 12

Correct answer D.
(1 mark)

e If your knowledge is sound you will quickly realise that this is human resource planning.

Question 13

Correct answer A.
(1 mark)

e The skills and abilities of the workforce are normally improved through training.

Question 14

Correct answer A.
(1 mark)

e Working conditions are a hygiene factor, so A is the correct answer.

Question 15

Correct answer C.
(1 mark)

e Autonomous work groups relates to team-working and is a non-financial method of motivation, whereas the other options are financial methods.

Short-answer questions (AS and A-level)

1 **Distinguish between quality control and quality assurance.** (3 marks)

e This effectively means 'define each of the terms thereby showing how they are different'.

> **Student A**
>
> Quality control involves inspecting products at the end of the production process, whereas quality assurance is self-checking by employees at every stage of the production process.

e **3/3 marks awarded.** A clear and concise answer — full marks.

> **Student B**
>
> Quality control is inspectors checking quality, whereas quality assurance is employees checking it.

e **1/3 marks awarded.** This answer is a little vague. There is some limited understanding, so perhaps 1 mark.

2 **Outline the difference between cash flow and profit.** (3 marks)

e The difference can be demonstrated by defining each term.

> **Student A**
>
> Cash flow shows the money coming into a business and the money going out of a business, whereas profit is the difference between revenue and costs.

e **3/3 marks awarded.** A clear, concise answer from this student.

> **Student B**
>
> Cash flow is money going into and out of a business, whereas profit is what is left over at the end.

e **2/3 marks awarded.** This answer demonstrates some basic understanding.

3 **What is meant by the human resource objective of diversity?** (3 marks)

e All that is required is a definition, in this case of diversity.

> **Student A**
>
> Diversity refers to the fact that although people are different in terms of race, religion, sex, age, etc., all should have equal access to employment and organisations must make sure all employees are aware of their rights regarding equality and diversity.

e **3/3 marks awarded.** This student has a clear understanding of diversity.

0/3 marks awarded. This student does not understand the term.

4 **Explain briefly why flexibility and dependability of suppliers are important operational targets.**

(3 marks)

 The key word here is 'briefly', so all that is needed is one sentence to demonstrate an understanding of the terms and another sentence or two to say why they are important to a business.

Student A

Flexibility and dependability refer to how reliable a particular supplier is in meeting a business's supply needs. This is important as a business does not want to run out of stock or carry too much stock. Both of these situations would end up costing the business money and therefore reduce profitability.

 3/3 marks awarded. This answer demonstrates a sound understanding of the terms and clearly explains why they are important to a business.

Student B

Flexibility is where a supplier can easily increase or decrease supplies without causing a problem, whereas dependability is always being able to supply and not letting a business down.

 2/3 marks awarded. This demonstrates an understanding of the terms, but there is no attempt to explain their importance.

5 **Explain the drawbacks of break-even analysis to a business operating in a competitive market.**

(5 marks)

 Although the question asks for drawbacks, it is not necessary to identify all of them — explaining one or two is sufficient to gain full marks.

Student A

A drawback of break-even analysis is that it is only really suitable for a one-product firm. Also, in a highly competitive market it is unlikely that a business will sell all its products and it would be unlikely for all of the products to be sold at the same price. This makes break-even analysis less useful as it assumes all products are sold and at the same price. In order to compete effectively in such a market, it is likely that the business will have regular offers and promotions, resulting in variable prices.

 5/5 marks awarded. A good answer. Various drawbacks are identified and that of pricing is clearly linked (applied) to a competitive market.

Student B

There are a number of drawbacks to break-even analysis. First, it is only really useful for a firm that makes one product. Secondly, it assumes that all products are sold and, thirdly, it assumes that they are all sold at the same price. The second two things are unlikely in practice.

@ **2/5 marks awarded.** This student simply outlines the various drawbacks of break-even analysis and there is no attempt to apply this to the competitive market situation.

6 Analyse the factors a UK business manufacturing high quality fabrics might consider before deciding to outsource production. (9 marks)

@ To be analytical, an answer needs to demonstrate a chain of argument — in this case, on the factors to be considered when outsourcing. To achieve full marks, the answer must also be in the context of a firm producing high quality fabrics.

Student A

A business may outsource production when it has insufficient capacity itself to complete its orders. This means that it secures the services of another business to undertake production.

In terms of fabrics, it would probably be fairly easy to find another manufacturer, especially if the business looks overseas. However, this business is producing high quality fabrics, so it is essential that any outsourced organisation is able to produce the same quality otherwise the business could easily find its sales fall and its reputation is damaged. If it chose an overseas producer, the business would need to make sure that its employment practices were up to standard as, again, if it was found to be using sweatshop labour its reputation for high quality could easily be tarnished. As a UK manufacturer, it may be that 'made in the UK' is a USP for the business, making the location of any outsourced producer important — if its products are made elsewhere, this could also damage its reputation.

Reliability and flexibility of an outsourced producer may be important as the manufacturer would want to make sure that any orders arrive on time and, where necessary, respond to changes in demand at short notice.

@ **9/9 marks awarded.** A good answer that is clearly applied to the aspect of high quality fabrics. The main argument relates to the reputation of this business, which is well developed. It considers the use of an overseas producer, which might damage any 'made in the UK' USP and whose employment practices might be poor. The final paragraph, although relevant, adds nothing in terms of marks as there is enough already for full marks.

Student B

There are a number of factors that a manufacturer would wish to consider before deciding to outsource its products. First, might be the quality of the products as a producer would want to make sure that any other firm producing its goods was able to produce at the same standard.

A second factor might be that of reliability. Would the outsourced business be able to deliver on time? Would it be flexible to changes in orders? For example, if this is a seasonal good, could it increase production quickly if necessary?

Cost is also an important factor. Would the outsourced producer be able to produce at a cost that still enables a profit to be made? All these are important factors to consider before deciding to outsource any production.

e **3/9 marks awarded.** This student has identified a number of factors, but there is no attempt to apply these to the high quality UK fabrics manufacturer. The development of each factor is also limited. As a result, this answer would struggle to achieve more than 3 marks.

7 **Company Y plc is a highly innovative and successful business in a fast-growing market and has decided to raise new capital to finance further growth through a share issue. Analyse the possible factors it may have considered in the decision to use share capital rather than loans.** (9 marks)

e It is important to recognise that this question is not only about the advantages of share capital as a source of funds; it is about why an innovative business in a growing market might choose this form of finance.

Student A

Share capital is an external source of long-term finance and has the benefits of not having to be paid back and no interest payments — a dividend may be given, but this is paid from profit. The other source of long-term finance is loan capital, but this has to be paid back and there is a cost in terms of interest. There are a number of reasons why this business may have chosen to use share capital.

The directors may have looked at the potential interest from investors in buying shares. As it is a highly innovative, successful business, it is likely to be profitable. This means that potential investors would be interested in buying shares. If the company continues to be innovative and profitable, not only would the share price increase but also there would be the prospect of dividend payments. The appetite of investors for shares would make this a good choice and avoid interest payments and having to pay back the money, which would be the case for a loan.

The business would also have looked at its capital structure and gearing. It may be that it already has a large amount of borrowing and wishes to avoid further loans. As it is a growing market, it may have used loans for expansion in the past. If it is now successful as a result of past investment, it would be better to use share capital.

e **9/9 marks awarded.** An excellent answer that is fully considered and in the context of a successful and innovative business. Although the final paragraph is relevant, it adds little in terms of marks as by this stage this answer has already achieved full marks.

Student B

The reason this business will have chosen share capital is because of the advantages it has over loan capital. Share capital does not have to be paid back and there is no interest to pay on it. A dividend is paid only to shareholders if a profit has been made and then only if the directors decide to give one. This is a big advantage to the business because if they use loan capital they would have to pay it back and they would have to pay interest. This could be difficult for them if they were struggling to make a profit or interest rates increase.

The business may also have looked at its current capital structure. What do they have in the way of loans at the moment? If they already have a great deal of loans, it would be wise not to have more. It might be that the business is already profitable and investors might be keen to buy shares in the company to benefit from future growth.

e **4/9 marks awarded.** This student has simply addressed the advantages of share capital as opposed to loan capital. There has been no attempt to apply this to the context of a successful, innovative business. Although there is some development of the arguments, the lack of application restricts the marks considerably.

Data-response questions (AS and A-level)

Question 1 Peter's Preserves plc

Peter Osman started his business 15 years ago as a small, family-run business making jams and jellies using his own unique recipes and locally grown fruits. He quickly established a reputation for high quality products that became so popular he was able to expand into a national business. The high-end customers he targets like his flexibility and his willingness to experiment with different preserves. As a result, he has been able to extend his product range to include more exotic preserves such as tomato and chilli, and gooseberry and mint, among others. This has been further supported by a series of cookbooks with Peter's products featuring in all the recipes.

On the surface everything looks perfect, but for Peter there are serious concerns:
- production is approaching full capacity at 95%
- labour productivity is declining

- there have been issues with quality and wastage is increasing
- there have been difficulties with the supply chain

Peter is well aware of the cause of some of these problems — to some extent caused by the tremendous growth of the business in a relatively short period of time. He not only needs more production capacity to cope with the increasing demand, but more efficient capacity. Up until now, his operation has been relatively labour-intensive and moving to a more capital-intensive approach would, he feels, go a long way to solving the first three problems. However, problems with the supply chain are more worrying.

Some key decisions are required over the coming months if Peter is to maintain the reputation of the business and continue to grow.

(a) Using figures to illustrate, explain how a figure of 95% capacity utilisation has been arrived at. (6 marks)

e This question requires students to demonstrate their understanding of capacity utilisation by creating their own figures to arrive at an answer of 95% capacity utilisation.

(b) Analyse the possible consequences for Peter's Preserves of continuing issues with quality. (9 marks)

e 'Analyse' means to develop a detailed line of argument in an answer. It is important to remember that any argument made should be specifically in relation to the consequences or impacts on Peter's Preserves.

(c) Analyse the factors that Peter might consider in making a decision to move to a more capital-intensive production process. (9 marks)

e Again, a detailed line of argument needs to be established in relation to Peter's Preserves. Although the question stipulates more than one factor, the focus should be on the depth of argument and not trying to identify multiple factors.

(d) To what extent is quality likely to be the most important consideration for Peter when choosing a supplier? (16 marks)

e This question asks for a judgement to be made and in writing an answer all skills should be covered: application, analysis and evaluation. As a result, detailed lines of argument should be established in the context of Peter's Preserves, arriving at a final conclusion as to whether or not quality is the most important consideration.

Student A

(a) Capacity utilisation is calculated using the following formula:

$$\frac{\text{actual output}}{\text{maximum possible output}} \times 100$$

The following calculation illustrates how a 95% figure was arrived at. If output is 95m jars and maximum capacity is 100m jars:

$$= \frac{95}{100} \times 100$$

= 95% capacity utilisation

ⓔ **6/6 marks awarded.** A complete answer. The correct formula has been identified, appropriate figures have been selected and these have been calculated correctly to achieve the answer of 95%.

(b) Quality is an important issue for any business as it can act as a USP. If the business produces high quality goods, this can avoid the costs associated with poor quality. This is particularly true for Peter as part of the reason for his success has been the high quality of his products and customer service. If these were to decline, it could lead to fewer orders and a deterioration not only of quality but also of the whole business performance. His products are more exclusive and aimed at high-end retailers where quality and service are essential to sales. Associated with the issue of quality is that of increasing wastage, which could further damage Peter's reputation with retailers and result in higher costs for the business, leading to lower profitability. This wastage might be in the production process or in returned items, all of which add to costs and make it more difficult to succeed in this particular market. All in all, quality is a big problem for Peter which he needs to resolve.

ⓔ **9/9 marks awarded.** This answer correctly identifies issues such as damage to reputation and rising costs and develops them in the context of Peter's preserves. Interestingly, rather than start a new paragraph when looking at wastage, this student links it to the previous issue of damaged reputation, thereby strengthening the overall depth of argument (analysis).

(c) By moving from a labour-intensive to a more capital-intensive business, Peter would be placing a greater reliance on machinery in production than labour. He may decide to do this because of the issues arising with labour productivity, quality and wastage (operational problems). These are important factors. Peter's Preserves has grown into a national business and, with increasing demand there is increasing pressure, which may be felt by the employees who are operating at very close to maximum capacity (95%). A more capital-intensive approach might relieve some of this pressure on capacity as capacity might be increased by the introduction of technology and labour productivity is also likely to increase. In addition, with machinery/technology the quality is likely to be more consistent and the current problems with wastage should be reduced. These are all important considerations that Peter will need to consider as he wants the business to be better able to meet the growing demands and to be able to overcome the current operational problems.

ℯ 9/9 marks awarded. This is a good answer that is set fully in the context of Peter's business and has a developed line of argument.

(d) A number of factors are likely to be taken into consideration when choosing a supplier and not just quality. Reliability, flexibility and payment terms are all important considerations. For Peter, quality will be of some importance as he is producing a high quality product, but it may not be the most important. We are told the business is experiencing problems with its supply chain. This could mean that there have been problems getting supplies on time or maybe the supplier has not been flexible to changes in demand: both are quite likely considering the growth of the business. Reliability and flexibility are important considerations as the business wants to maintain its high reputation for customer service. If Peter cannot get deliveries out to customers on time because of problems with suppliers, this could damage his reputation and result in lower orders in the future.

Overall, quality is a consideration for Peter but it may not be the most important factor. This is because, when choosing a supplier, a range of factors needs to be considered. In Peter's case reliability and flexibility of the supplier are likely to be just as important. Other factors such as price and payment terms may also be considered, although in Peter's case these may be of less importance.

ℯ 16/16 marks awarded. This is a good answer that addresses the specific question set. It is fully in context and the arguments are well developed in supporting the conclusion that quality may not be the most important factor.

ℯ Total score: 40/40 marks = a top grade A. Overall, this student has provided an excellent response that should easily achieve the top grade.

Student B

(a) Capacity utilisation refers to the amount of total capacity that is currently being used. It is calculated using the following formula:

$$\frac{\text{output}}{\text{maximum output}} \times 100$$

ℯ 2/6 marks awarded. This student has correctly identified the formula but has been unable to follow this up with the relevant calculation needed.

(b) Quality can act as a USP for a business, which gives a reason for customers to purchase one product rather than another. This seems to be the case for Peter, so if his quality declines then his reputation would be harmed and there would be fewer reasons for customers to buy his product. As a result, he could see sales decline and profit fall. This would not be good for his business, especially if he wishes to grow further in the future.

Quality issues can increase the costs of a business. This might be because of returned goods or wastage on the production line. Again, these are likely to increase the costs of the business and result in lower profitability, which could damage any ambitions he has for further growth.

e **4/9 marks awarded.** This student has correctly identified the problems associated with poor quality, but has not set the development of problems in the context of Peter's business and therefore misses out on application marks. The depth of development (analysis) is limited by the fact that reputation and wastage are dealt with as two separate points (paragraphs) rather than trying to link them together as Student A did.

(c) Capital-intensive production means a business has a greater reliance on machinery and technology in production rather than labour. Before deciding on a more capital-intensive approach, Peter may have considered the following factors such as the cost of machinery, the impact on the efficiency of the business and how it might affect the nature of the business.

At the moment, the business is suffering from declining efficiency as labour productivity is falling. There are also problems with wastage and quality. Becoming more capital-intensive would enable the business to produce more products with less labour, thereby improving productivity. Quality would also probably be more consistent and as a result wastage could be reduced. As the business is experiencing increasing demand, it is possible only a few employees would need to be made redundant and they could just be redeployed. These are all factors that Peter might need to consider.

e **5/9 marks awarded.** The first paragraph identifies a number of relevant factors (content only). The second paragraph tries to develop the factors of improved efficiency and quality and raises the impact on employees. There is some attempt to develop the points and set them in the context of the business, but overall the answer lacks real depth of analysis.

(d) A business normally considers a number of factors when choosing a supplier. Quality would be important to Peter as he is producing a high quality product and it goes without saying that supplies need to be high quality.

He would also have to consider price and payment terms. There is no point paying over the top prices just to get good quality as this could ruin the business. Payment terms might be important in that Peter may be able to negotiate lengthy credit terms with one supplier, whereas another may want payment almost immediately.

Peter would also want a supplier who could deliver on time and be able to be flexible to changes in demand. This could be crucial as it is likely that demand will fluctuate at different times of year. As a result, he may have to give a little in terms of quality in order to get a supplier who is dependable.

Overall, although quality is an important consideration, it is a combination of factors that determines the choice.

ⓔ 7/16 marks awarded. This student has made the mistake of trying to cover as many points as possible. As a result, none is fully developed (analysis) and in this answer they are not set in the context of Peter's Preserves (application). There is a judgement made, but it is not fully supported in the context of this particular business.

ⓔ Total score: 18/40 marks = a low pass grade. Overall, this student has produced a weak response that might achieve a grade E but no more.

Question 2 Company Z plc

The following information relates to Company Z.

	June £m	July £m	August £m	September £m	October £m	November £m
Cash in						
Sales	12.5	13.5	14.0	13.0	12.0	10.0
Cash out						
Materials	7.5	8.1	8.4	8.4	**B**	7.0
Labour	4.0	4.0	4.0	4.0	4.0	4.0
Administration	0.5	0.5	0.5	0.5	0.5	0.5
Other costs	0.5	0.5	0.5	0.5	1.0	0.5
Total	12.5	13.1	13.4	13.4	13.6	12.0
Net cash flow	0	**A**	0.6	(0.4)	(1.6)	(2.0)
Opening balance	0.7	0.7	1.1	1.7	1.3	(0.3)
Closing balance	0.7	1.1	1.7	1.3	(0.3)	**C**

Figure 1 A cash flow forecast

Revenue	£160m
Fixed costs	£15m
Variable costs	£140m
Output	8m
Price elasticity	−0.7

Table 1 Financial data

Equity	£30m
Loans	£20m

Table 2 Capital structure

Return on investment	10%
Operating profit margin	5%

Table 3 Financial objectives

Company Z has an excellent reputation for the high quality of its product and customer service. This enables it to compete successfully in a competitive market. However, it does suffer on account of the nature of its product (which is seasonal) and it has to make use of a sizable overdraft to overcome the resulting cash flow problems. In order to overcome this problem of seasonality, it wishes to raise further finance to expand production capacity. The extra capacity would enable the company to successfully target markets overseas, resulting in more even production throughout the year. A key decision now is how the business will raise the additional capital needed.

(a) Work out the three missing figures (**A**, **B** and **C**) in the cash flow forecast. (3 marks)

e All this question requires is the calculation of the missing figures in the cash flow statement.

(b) (i) What is the formula for return on investment? (2 marks)

(ii) Calculate Company Z's operating profit margin. (4 marks)

(iii) Calculate Company Z's capital gearing. (4 marks)

(iv) Calculate Company Z's break-even output. (4 marks)

ⓔ With questions such as this, it is wise to identify the formula and show all calculations as marks will be awarded for each stage of the process.

(c) Explain why raising the price of its product might be the best way for Company Z to raise its operating profit margin. (4 marks)

ⓔ The command word 'explain' indicates that the answer should be addressed specifically in relation to Company Z.

(d) Analyse the reasons why an overdraft may have been the best way of overcoming Company Z's cash flow problems. (9 marks)

ⓔ The command word here is 'analyse' and as a result an in-depth line of argument is required to explain why an overdraft may have been the best way for Company Z to overcome its cash flow problems.

(e) To what extent do you believe that taking out a further loan is the best way for Company Z to raise the finance needed? (15 marks)

ⓔ 'To what extent' means a judgement has to be made, in other words is a loan the best way for Company Z to raise further finance? Lines of argument might be developed in detail both for and against a loan and a final conclusion drawn.

Student A

(a) **A** = £400,000; **B** = £8.1m; **C** = −£2.3m.

ⓔ **3/3 marks awarded.** All correct for 1 mark each.

(b) (i)

$$\text{Return on investment} = \frac{\text{net profit}}{\text{amount invested}} \times 100$$

ⓔ **2/2 marks awarded.** An accurate formula.

(ii)

$$\text{Operating profit margin} = \frac{\text{operating profit}}{\text{Sales revenue}} \times 100$$

$$= \frac{5}{160} \times 100$$

$$= 3.125\%$$

ⓔ **4/4 marks awarded.** Correctly calculated.

(iii)

$$\text{Capital gearing} = \frac{\text{loan capital}}{\text{total capital employed}} \times 100$$

$$= \frac{20}{50} \times 100$$

$$= 40\%$$

🟢 **4/4 marks awarded.** Correctly calculated.

(iv) Break-even output $= \dfrac{\text{fixed costs}}{\text{contribution per unit}}$

To calculate contribution per unit:

$$\frac{\text{sales revenue} - \text{variable costs}}{\text{output}}$$

$$= \frac{160 - 140}{8}$$

$$= \text{£}2.5$$

Therefore, break-even output is:

$$\frac{15m}{2.5}$$

$$= 6m \text{ units}$$

🟢 **4/4 marks awarded.** Correctly calculated.

(c) In order to improve profit margins, a business might either reduce costs or raise prices. In the case of Company Z, raising price may be the best option as it has a reputation for high quality products and customer service, which means customers may be prepared to pay more to receive this product. This is most likely to be the case as demand for the product is shown to be relatively price inelastic at −0.7. Raising prices, therefore, would most likely improve the operating profit margin.

🟢 **4/4 marks awarded.** A good answer, set fully in the context of Company Z.

(d) An overdraft is an arrangement with a bank whereby a business can spend more than it has in its bank account, up to a preset limit. The great advantage of this arrangement is its flexibility and the fact that interest is only charged on the amount overdrawn. This is likely to be the best arrangement for Company Z in terms of its cash flow problems for a number of reasons. The first is the nature of the business, which is seasonal. Looking at the cash flow forecast, it is only likely to require this money during the off-season. During the peak season, Company Z would not need to draw on the overdraft and therefore would not have to pay any interest. Added to this is the fact that it wants to expand overseas in order to overcome this seasonality, so the need for an overdraft may be only temporary. Other options such as trying to extend its credit period or shortening customers' credit period could damage relationships with suppliers or customers and impact on the company's high reputation. As a result, in the case of Company Z, an overdraft would probably be the best option.

ⓔ 9/9 marks awarded. This student provides a response that is fully focused on the question. An overdraft is defined and the benefits are clearly developed in the context of Company Z.

(e) Company Z is looking to raise long-term finance for expansion and probably has two options open to it. It can raise new share capital or obtain a loan from a bank. A loan would be a possibility as at the moment gearing is only 40% and, for example, a £10m loan would only increase this to 50%. The extra interest payments of, say, £1m (10% on £10m loan) could easily be covered from its current profit of £5m. If, as expected, the expansion creates further sales, it is likely that profit will increase and the need for an overdraft might be reduced, leading to lower costs and further increasing profit.

The alternative to a loan would be new share capital, which has the great advantage of not having to be paid back and having no interest payments. As a successful company with a good reputation, it is likely that new shares would be in demand but existing shareholders might be a little upset as their own holdings become diluted and any dividends in the future might fall. However, if the business is successful, both share value and dividend could rise.

Overall, this business seems to be in the enviable position of being able to use either method for new capital. Whether or not loans are the best option depends on how much is needed and the objectives of the board and whether they wish further dilution in terms of a share issue. If that is not the case and the amount is not too great, loan capital would be the best option.

ⓔ 15/15 marks awarded. An excellent answer with well-developed arguments set in the context of Company Z. The final conclusion is also well considered, resulting in full marks.

ⓔ Total score: 45/45 marks = a top grade A. It is difficult to fault this student, who gives an excellent answer that would have no problem achieving a top grade.

Student B

(a) **A** = 0.4; **B** = 8.1; **C** = −2.3.

ⓔ 0/3 marks awarded. Although this student probably believes these figures have been calculated correctly, they have overlooked the fact that the figures in the data are in millions of pounds — a common oversight and in this case resulting in no marks.

(b) (i) Return on investment = ?

e **0/2 marks awarded.** This student has clearly not learnt this formula.

(ii) Operating profit margin = 160 – 15 – 140

$$= £5m$$

e **1/4 marks awarded.** Although a correct profit figure has been calculated, this student has not learnt the formula for operating profit.

(iii) Capital gearing = ?

e **0/4 marks awarded.** Again, a lack of detailed learning has cost marks.

(iv) Break-even output $= \dfrac{\text{fixed costs}}{\text{contribution per unit}}$

$$= \frac{15}{?} = ?$$

e **1/4 marks awarded.** On this occasion the correct formula has been learnt, but this student is unsure of how to calculate contribution per unit.

(c) Increasing price is the best way to improve operating profit margin as with a higher price the business will receive more revenue which would go towards increasing the profit margin. This is providing consumers are prepared to pay the price — they may do so in this case as Company Z has a high quality product.

e **1/4 marks awarded.** This is a rather weak answer. There is some understanding of why raising price might increase profit, but it is poorly developed in the context of Company Z. There is just a passing reference to the high quality product. If this had been linked to price inelasticity, a much higher mark would have been achieved.

(d) An overdraft is an extension on a business current account which allows it to spend more than it has in the account up to a set limit. This is a short-term arrangement with its bank and has the advantage of only being charged interest on the amount overdrawn. Therefore, this would be better than a loan as interest is paid on the loan throughout the whole period it is borrowed.

An alternative might be for the business to collect in quicker any money it is owed or it could delay some of its own payments. Both these methods would help to improve the cash flow position, but it might upset those it is dealing with.

Overall, an overdraft is likely to be the best way to overcome cash flow problems, especially considering almost all businesses run an overdraft anyway.

ⓔ 3/9 marks awarded. Although this student understands what an overdraft is and how it and other methods might be used to overcome cash flow problems, the answer is not set in the context of Company Z. There is some development (analysis) of why an overdraft might be better than a loan, but that is all.

> **(e)** I don't think a loan is the best way for Company Z to raise new capital. This is because a loan needs to be paid back and interest has to be paid on the amount borrowed. This could add high costs to the business and, if interest rates increased over time, this could put the business under real pressure.
>
> A better option might be new share capital as this does not have to be paid back and there are no interest payments. Dividends are only paid out of profit so this would be a much better option for the company. The only problem might be existing shareholders might feel they will lose out as they might get less dividend in the future.
>
> A third option for the business might be retained profit. Company Z made £5m last year and this might go some way towards the sum needed. The great advantage of this is there are no costs with it at all.
>
> Overall, the best way is likely to be share capital and retained profit rather than loan capital as it does not have to be paid back or have interest payments.

ⓔ 8/15 marks awarded. This student has a good understanding of the various ways of raising long-term capital and there is some development (analysis) of the benefits and drawbacks of the various methods. Although there is a little context, both it and the arguments made lack real depth. There is some support for the judgement made, making this overall a reasonable answer, but a little more context and depth of argument could have made it a good answer.

ⓔ Total score: 14/45 marks = a weak response that would struggle to achieve a pass grade.

Question 3 Gallagher's Ales plc

Sam Gallagher is chairman and managing director of Gallagher's Ales plc, a national drinks manufacturer providing a range of ales and soft drinks to over 1,000 pubs and retailers nationwide. However, recently things have started to go wrong in the distribution section of the business, as shown by the data in Table 1.

Increase in customer complaints	50% increase in the last 12 months
Labour retention	Fallen by 20% in the last 12 months
Labour turnover	Increased 45% in the last 12 months

Table 1 Data on Gallagher's Ales

This deterioration in data seems to coincide with the employment of a new manager in the distribution section whose style of management is autocratic and 'hard'. However, the reason he was appointed was because of a deteriorating position in the section, but clearly this had not worked.

Sam is now contemplating a much more radical approach to the problem. He wants to have a complete overhaul of the section, with jobs redesigned to make them more rewarding. Under the present system, customers phone in their orders and the calls are answered by the first available telephonist, who sends through the order to the warehouse where lorries are loaded for delivery. Once loaded, any one of 24 drivers then makes the delivery. Sam wants to divide the section into teams, with telephonists, warehousemen and drivers in a team servicing a specific group of customers. By doing this, customers should benefit from dealing with the same people each time they make an order and it would be delivered by a regular driver. As a result, employees will get to know each customer's requirements and be able to anticipate their needs, as well as feeling a sense of responsibility towards them. It might also enable greater involvement in decision-making, as employees may then be able to identify areas for further improvement and have a better idea of likely demand, enabling more efficient stock control.

Although there appears to be some initial opposition from the workforce, Sam is hopeful that they will come round and that significant improvements in customer complaints, labour retention and turnover can be made.

(a) State how the figures for the following would have been calculated.

    (i) Increase in customer complaints.   (2 marks)

    (ii) Labour retention.   (2 marks)

    (iii) Labour turnover.   (2 marks)

ⓔ This question simply requires an identification of the formula or method of calculation.

(b) Explain the potential drawbacks to Gallagher's Ales of a hard approach to human relations.   (5 marks)

ⓔ The command word 'explain' indicates that it is just application that is required and the key to achieving this is to link the drawbacks directly to Gallagher's Ales by using evidence from the information given.

(c) Analyse how the Hackman and Oldham model can be applied to support the changes proposed by Sam.   (9 marks)

ⓔ A developed argument is required here to demonstrate how this model can be applied directly to Gallagher's Ale's situation and the changes proposed.

(d) Evaluate the extent to which you believe Sam's idea to move to team-working has been influenced by the theories of either Herzberg or Maslow. (15 marks)

ⓔ 'Evaluate' means that a judgement needs to be made, in other words an extended argument needs to be made either supporting or rejecting the view that the chosen theory can be linked with team-working. This might be achieved by looking at both sides of the argument and then drawing an overall conclusion.

(e) To what extent do you believe the introduction of team-working will lead to significant improvements in the problems in the distribution section? (15 marks)

ⓔ Although team-working is an aspect of both parts (d) and (e), they require totally different answers. The focus of this question is the problems within the distribution section of the business and an argument needs to be fully developed and in context as to whether a move to team-working will overcome the problems.

Student A

(a) **(i)** Increase in customer complaints $= \dfrac{\text{difference between number of complaints this year and last year}}{\text{number of complaints last year}} \times 100$

(ii) Labour retention $= \dfrac{\text{number of employees employed for more than 1 year}}{\text{total number of employees}} \times 100$

(iii) Labour turnover $= \dfrac{\text{number of employees who have left during the year}}{\text{total number of employees}} \times 100$

ⓔ **6/6 marks awarded.** All correct for 2 marks each.

(b) A hard approach to management is one where workers are given very little say in what they are doing and the manager tends to be autocratic in their approach. Such an approach can upset workers and lead to a lack of motivation and poor performance. This seems to be the case with the new manager who was brought into the distribution department. Although there were problems before his appointment, the increasing complaints, lower labour retention rate and rising labour turnover illustrate the likely drawbacks resulting from a hard approach to human relations.

ⓔ **5/5 marks awarded.** A good answer. An understanding of a hard approach to management is demonstrated and set in the context of Gallagher's Ales.

(c) The Hackman and Oldham model looks at work from the point of view of three characteristics: the core job dimensions, the psychological states and the outcomes. Working backwards in the model, management would like the following outcomes: motivation of the workforce, improved performance, satisfaction and low absenteeism/turnover. These outcomes are more likely to be achieved if the following psychological states are present: the work is meaningful, workers have responsibility for the outcomes and have knowledge of the results. This is more likely to be achieved if, in the characteristics of the job, there is skill and task variety as well as significance, workers have autonomy and are given feedback.

When looking at the changes proposed at Gallagher's, it does appear that they fit neatly into this model in many ways. As workers will be organised into teams dealing with a set group of customers, there is a much greater significance to the work, they also have autonomy over what they are doing and they will get direct feedback. As a result, responsibility will increase and the work will become more meaningful. It is yet to be seen whether these changes will improve motivation, job satisfaction and performance, but the likelihood is they will. It therefore does seem that the model can be easily applied to and support the changes made.

🄴 **9/9 marks awarded.** This is an interesting question that addresses some new content in this specification. This student demonstrates a full understanding of the Hackman and Oldham model and clearly links how it relates to and supports the changes made at Gallagher's.

(d) Herzberg put forward a two-factor theory where he considered hygiene factors and motivating factors. Hygiene factors themselves, such as good working conditions and pay, do not motivate; however they do need to be present. Motivators were things like involvement in decision-making, responsibility and recognition. By introducing team-working it would appear that Sam is trying to incorporate these motivating factors into the work being done. Jobs will be redesigned to make them more rewarding. Workers will have responsibility for the efficient delivery of supplies, whereas before no one could be held responsible. There is now also the opportunity for feedback and involvement of workers in the decision-making approach, whereas before the hard approach to human resources would have discouraged this.

The above seem to suggest that Sam may well have been influenced by the theory of Herzberg as he appears to have been trying to create a situation where motivating factors are present. In practice, however, many managers have probably never studied the work of Herzberg and rarely read up on theories of management in order to develop changes to work practice. Overall, therefore, although these changes appear to fit the theory nicely, Sam is probably only trying to look for new ways of motivating. Perhaps he had seen a similar system elsewhere or just felt it was a good idea, rather than trying to specifically apply a theory.

🄴 **15/15 marks awarded.** This is well thought-out (planned) answer, finishing with a considered conclusion. A clear understanding of Herzberg's theory is demonstrated and an argument is developed applying the changes made by Sam to the theory. A conclusion is then drawn and supported, suggesting that managers rarely base changes on a specific theory.

(e) The problems in the distribution section are related to customer complaints, labour retention and labour turnover. These probably stemmed from the lack of coordination in the section. No one could be held responsible, work lacked meaningfulness and the number of complaints would have just left workers feeling incapable of making things better. Team-working would certainly change some of this as each team is responsible for a specific group of customers. These customers will deal with the same people each time an order is made, resulting in a more meaningful relationship between workers and customers. As a result, workers will hopefully come to have a sense of responsibility toward their customers and look to develop and improve that relationship. The various jobs in each team will become more meaningful, have greater involvement in the decision-making process and there will be a much greater sense of responsibility. Done properly, customer complaints should significantly reduce, making the work more rewarding and reducing labour turnover and hopefully increasing labour retention.

Overall, providing there are no underlying issues within the business such as the current manager with his hard approach to human relations, adopting team-working should go some way to overcoming the problems within the distribution section.

e **15/15 marks awarded.** Another well-considered answer that is focused specifically on the question set. Arguments are well developed and set in the context of the business and the conclusion is well supported.

e **Total score: 50/50 marks = a top grade A. This student has provided a consistently excellent response that would have little problem achieving a top grade.**

Student B

(a) (i)   Increase in customer complaints =

(ii) Labour retention =

(iii) Labour turnover = $\dfrac{\text{number leaving}}{\text{total employees}} \times 100$

e **2/6 marks awarded.** This student has failed to undertake the necessary learning, with only the last formula identified correctly.

(b) A hard approach to human relations tends to be autocratic in its approach and workers are given little involvement in the decision-making. As a result, they may lack motivation and performance may drop off. Involvement, recognition and responsibility are all motivating factors in Herzberg's theory and a hard approach tends to ignore these factors, supporting the view that workers lack motivation.

ⓔ **2/5 marks awarded.** This is a theoretical answer with no application to the context of the business. As a result, only content marks are awarded.

(c) The changes proposed at Gallagher's are that the workers' jobs will be redesigned to make them more rewarding. Under the present system, customers phone in their orders and they are answered by the first available telephonist, who sends through the order to the warehouse where lorries are loaded for delivery. Once loaded, any one of 24 drivers then makes the delivery. Sam proposes to change things so that workers are organised into teams, with telephonists, warehousemen and drivers in a team servicing a set group of customers. By doing this, customers should benefit from dealing with the same people each time they make an order and it will be delivered by a regular driver. As a result, employees will to know customer requirements and be able to anticipate their needs and feel a sense of responsibility towards them. Such changes seem to fit nicely into the Hackman and Oldham model.

ⓔ **0/9 marks awarded.** Clearly, this student does not understand the Hackman and Oldham model. Although they give the impression of understanding the changes made, in reality all they have done is repeat the text from the source material.

(d) Sam may well have tried to implement the theory of Herzberg. His theory is that some aspects of work act as hygiene factors whereas others act as motivators. The hygiene factors include such things as pay, holidays and other conditions of work, whereas the motivators include responsibility, recognition, status and involvement. By introducing team-working, it seems Sam is looking at the motivating factors because team-working gives responsibility to the team for successful completion of tasks. It also often creates greater involvement as the team can have input into the decision-making process. By providing greater scope for responsibility and involvement, it also creates a recognition for workers, giving them a feeling of status. As a result, I would say that Sam is hugely influenced by the Herzberg's theory when making these changes.

ⓔ **6/15 marks awarded.** This student provides a purely theoretical approach with no specific link or mention of the changes proposed by Sam. It is suggested that because the changes made seem to fit with Herzberg, Sam must have been influenced by it — a conclusion that lacks any support.

(e) Team-working is where workers are organised into groups to carry out a particular aspect of work. As a team they are normally responsible for what happens in this aspect and have a good deal of involvement in terms of decision-making, for example making improvements in this aspect of work. This gives a much greater sense of responsibility and recognition for the job being done and is likely to be motivating. This links into Herzberg's theory where he suggested there were hygiene and motivating factors. Responsibility, recognition and involvement are motivating factors, so if team working provides these then motivation should improve and as a result the problems should be overcome.

On the other hand, it may be that these workers just find the work boring and no matter what the business does they will not be motivated. Answering a telephone and driving a lorry are not very interesting jobs, so it may be difficult to motivate these workers.

Overall, however, I suggest the introduction of team-working will improve the performance of the distribution section.

e **6/15 marks awarded.** Although this student tries to look at both sides of the argument, there is no context (application). The argument made is a reasonable one, but without context it is difficult to make anything by way of supported judgement in this question.

e **Total score: 16/50 marks = a low pass grade. A weak response that would struggle to achieve a pass grade. The best that could be hoped for would be a grade E.**

AS case study

McNab's is renowned for producing some of the finest woollen and cashmere cloth, clothing and accessories. It has been in existence on the same site in Scotland for over 200 years and has established a reputation for the superior quality of its products with high-end retailers such as Burberry as customers. Although by far the biggest market is within the UK at around 65% of sales, the European market and Far Eastern markets are particularly strong.

Having performed particularly well in 2013 with a profit of just over £2.6m, the company has fallen into a loss. The relatively mild winter of the last 2 years has had a significant effect on sales, which were down almost 10% by value. This is largely caused by many of the customers ordering less stock because of carrying over stock from the previous year. The problem of falling sales has also not been helped by the continued economic problems that continue to exist in many of McNab's markets because of the recession, which it has still not fully recovered from.

The textile industry, like many others, has seen significant investment into technology in order to improve efficiency and competitiveness. Although McNab's reputation for superior quality and targeting of high-end customers has given it a USP, the company cannot afford to rely only on this. As a result, significant investment has taken place into state-of-the-art equipment, which has resulted in a fall in unit costs of production and a rise in productivity before 2013. This has all been largely financed by retained profit.

Despite job losses as a result of this investment, one of the features of McNab's over the years has been its excellent employer–employee relations. Its soft approach to human relations and good communication with employees through work councils are key features in this. In the current situation, this has been helped by the decision not to lay off any of its 800 workers despite the impact on gross profit margins and operational efficiencies. The board of directors are convinced that retaining key craft skills is far more important in their industry.

The board also believes that sales will soon pick up as McNab's products are aimed at high-end consumers who are perhaps affected less by recessionary pressure and more by quality. The brand and 'made in Scotland' USP are key factors that attract customers, resulting in a relatively inelastic demand. The company has also recently diversified its business somewhat to offer a café and shop on its factory site. This has become increasingly popular with locals and is now also a popular tourist attraction for visitors to Scotland, especially those from the Far East and America who are keen to spend and shop for the quality products on offer. As well as this, it has recently set up a Twitter account, which has quickly amassed a big following.

	2013 £ (m)	2014 £ (m)
Revenue	51.2	46.8
Gross profit	8.5	7.0
Operating profit	2.63	(1.8)

Table 1 Financial data

	2013	2014
Employee costs	£15.5m	£15.6m
Productivity	250	230
Employee costs as a % of turnover	30.27%	?
Labour turnover	5.5%	5.4%

Table 2 Data on McNab's

(a) Calculate the gross profit margin for 2014. (3 marks)

ⓔ Knowledge of a formula is required — in this case, gross profit as a percentage of turnover.

(b) Calculate employee costs as a % of turnover for 2014. (3 marks)

ⓔ Again, knowledge of the formula is essential for this calculation. Providing it has been learnt, this should not cause a problem.

(c) Explain what is meant by McNab's soft human relations approach. (4 marks)

ⓔ There are only 4 marks for this question, so a sentence outlining what is meant by a soft approach and another sentence relating this to McNab's should be sufficient.

(d) Analyse the importance of brand image to the success of McNab's. (9 marks)

ⓔ As this is an analysis question, a developed line of argument is required suggesting why brand image is important to McNab's.

(e) Analyse the benefits for McNab's of financing investment through retained profit. (9 marks)

ⓔ Again, a developed line of argument is requirement, this time addressing the benefits of retained profit as a source of capital for investment. Any argument must be linked directly to McNab's in order to achieve full marks.

(f) Discuss the extent to which the investment in technology is key to McNab's competitiveness. (16 marks)

ⓔ This question requires a judgement. When answering it is wise to create some balance, so perhaps look at why technology may be key, then give the reasons why it may not be important and then finally come to your overall judgement.

(g) To what extent do you believe the directors of McNab's are correct in their decision not to lay off workers as a result of falling demand? (16 marks)

ⓔ Again, balance required here, so an approach looking at the reasons in support of the decision and then the reasons against, and finally your overall judgement, would be a sensible approach.

(h) To what extent do you believe external factors are the main contributor to the falling profitability performance of McNab's? (20 marks)

ⓔ As with the parts (f) and (g), this answer should have balance, looking at both sides of the argument before coming to your overall judgement.

A further point regarding the last three questions: your marks will not be determined by the number of reasons you can identify both for and against a particular point of view. Examiners are looking for developed lines of arguments made in the context of the case study (in this case, McNab's). Often one argument for and one against a particular view, plus a supported judgement, are sufficient.

Student A

(a) Gross profit margin for 2014 $= \dfrac{\text{gross profit}}{\text{revenue}} \times 100$

$\qquad\qquad = \dfrac{7}{46.8} \times 100$

$\qquad\qquad = 14.96\%$

ⓔ **3/3 marks awarded.** Correct answer for full marks.

(b) Employee costs as % turnover for 2014 $= \dfrac{\text{employee costs}}{\text{turnover}} \times 100$

$\qquad\qquad = \dfrac{15.6}{46.8} \times 100$

$\qquad\qquad = 33.33\%$

ⓔ **3/3 marks awarded.** Correct answer for full marks.

(c) A soft approach to human relations is one where workers are treated with respect. They are treated as an important asset to the business, with their welfare and motivation being crucial. This is demonstrated in McNab's by its good communication and relations with the workforce and its decision not to lay off workers.

ⓔ **4/4 marks awarded.** A good answer, short and to the point, which is important in this case study question paper as there is a lot to get through in the time available.

(d) Brand image is related to how the business is perceived by customers and can be important to the success of the business. Brand image can act as a USP and this is probably the case for McNab's. Not only is the company viewed as high quality — selling in high-end retailers such as Burberry — but it also has a 'made in Scotland' tag. These two factors combined mean that consumers are prepared to the pay the relatively high prices, resulting in a price inelastic product. This means that demand is relatively unaffected by changes in price — even if prices increase, the percentage change in demand would be less than the percentage change in price, resulting in higher revenue and profit. It is this perceived image of a high quality, 'made in Scotland' product that has created the inelastic demand and has been important in the success of McNab's.

ⓔ **9/9 marks awarded.** A well-developed answer that is fully in context (applied).

(e) Retained profit is that profit which is kept within the business for future investment. The great benefit of retained profit is that, unlike a bank loan, there are no interest charges and it does not have to be paid back. This is the most cost-effective way for any business, let alone McNab's, to finance capital investment. It is particularly important for McNab's as it is operating in uncertain times: 2014 saw a loss being made and, if it had taken out loans, this loss could have been higher because of interest payments. In the worst case scenario, a bank might even call in its loans, resulting in insolvency. Using retained profit also means the business is in a stronger position in terms of retaining employees. If it had used loan finance, this may have been more difficult because of the pressure on costs. Retained profit, therefore, has a number of benefits as a source of long-term capital investment for McNab's.

ⓔ **9/9 marks awarded.** An excellent answer demonstrating a well-developed argument (analysis) that is fully in context (application).

(f) Investment in technology is likely to improve the competitiveness of McNab's, but it is unlikely to be the only way. Technology means that its goods can be produced more efficiently — more products from the same number of workers or the same number of products from fewer workers. This means, as stated, that unit costs are reduced and as a result prices may be reduced, making McNab's more competitive on price.

However, the company produces for high-end retailers such as Burberry, where price may be less important and perhaps quality and customer service are more important. Maintaining high quality standards may therefore be much more important to the competiveness of the business. Associated with this is the 'made in Scotland' theme, which sets it apart from other producers and gives it a competitive advantage.

Overall, therefore, technology may increase competitiveness but it may not be the only or best way to do so. The business needs to make sure that quality is maintained and the 'made in Scotland' theme is continued in order to improve competitiveness. In other words, an investment in technology will help its competitiveness, but it may not be the key to its competitiveness.

ⓔ **13/16 marks awarded.** This is a well-balanced answer that addresses the impact of technology on competitiveness and looks at other factors. It is clearly applied to the case and, although the arguments could have been developed a little more fully, the conclusion is well supported, making this a very good answer.

(g) The decision not to lay off workers has been a tricky one for McNab's and whether it was right or wrong in the end will probably depend on how long the dip in sales lasts. If it goes on for some time, the business may in the end have to make workers redundant.

On the face of it, however, this may well be a good decision. It is are operating in a market where quality is important and its products and production requires skilled workers. Labour retention is therefore important: if it were to lay off workers, they may not be available when demand picks up. This would result in the need to recruit and train new workers, which could be costly both in terms of actual costs and any costs related to the production problems and in terms of quality resulting from inexperienced workers.

At the moment, the company has good labour relations, which if it made redundancies could be affected. As all decisions are fully communicated with workers and their involvement is important, they are likely to be engaged and motivated. The labour turnover figure is also low at around 5% and these workers will want to do all they can to help the business through this difficult period.

Overall, in the short term this is probably a wise decision as labour costs as a percentage of turnover at the moment have increased by only around 3% and the business can probably cope with this. In the longer term, should demand fail to pick up this decision is likely to be unsustainable.

e 16/16 marks awarded. An excellent answer that has been carefully planned and leads to a considered conclusion. The arguments are well developed and fully in context, and the conclusion is well supported.

(h) A number of factors have affected the profitability of this business, of which external factors have been the main contributor. McNab's has been faced with falling demand because of the economic downturn, something that is beyond its control. This situation has been exacerbated by some mild winters, resulting again in lower demand for its cloth and woollens. Whereas its target market might have been less affected by the economic downturn, when this factor is combined with the mild winters there has been perhaps little that the business could do to avoid falling into a loss.

Despite the above, the business might have been able to do more to alleviate the situation. The decision by management not to lay off workers has meant the loss has been greater than it might otherwise have been. If labour costs as a percentage of turnover could have been kept at the 2013 figure, the loss could have been reduced by just over £1m. This decision by management has therefore had an impact on profitability.

Overall, however, although internal decisions have perhaps made the impact on profitability worse than it might otherwise have been, it is external factors that have been the primary cause of the decline in profitability.

e 18/20 marks awarded. This is another excellent answer from this student. It is well balanced, looking at both external and internal factors — they have done well to have spotted the internal factor in this case. The arguments are well developed and fully in context, and the final conclusion is fully supported by their answer.

e Total score: 75/80 marks = a top grade A. This is an excellent response overall that would have little problem achieving a grade A.

Questions & Answers

(a) Gross profit = 16%.

e **0/3 marks awarded.** It looks as though this student has used the figures for 2013, but having rounded their answer there is no way of telling for sure. If their working had been shown, it would have been possible to give 1 mark for the correct method (formula), but without working this is impossible.

(b) Employee costs as a % turnover = 30%.

e **0/3 marks awarded.** Again, it looks as though the wrong year has been used, the answer rounded and no working is shown.

(c) The characteristics of a soft human relations approach are that employees are treated as individuals and an asset to the business. As a result, their needs and motivation have a high priority. This approach is certainly evident at McNab's.

e **2/4 marks awarded.** Although a soft approach is understood, it has not been applied effectively to the McNab's case.

(d) Brand image refers to the way consumers see a product or service and can influence a consumer to purchase. For example, McDonald's has a well-recognised brand image for quality fast food and as a result consumers flock to their outlets. This generates high turnover and profit. If this image were to become tarnished as a result of poor quality from one of its franchised outlets, this would have a big impact on the whole business, leading to lower revenues and profit. Therefore, it can be seen that brand image is of crucial importance to a business and McNab's success will therefore be in the most part because of its well-known brand image.

e **4/9 marks awarded.** It looks as though this student might have previously answered a question on brand image relating to McDonald's and as a result they have failed to apply their answer to McNab's. There is some analysis, but the lack of application significantly reduces the mark gained.

(e) Retained profit is profit that is kept within the business and not given to shareholders as dividend. It can be used for investment into capital equipment. This would be a good way for McNab's to finance its new equipment as there is no interest to be paid and the money does not have to be paid back. If it had a loan, it would have to pay it back and pay interest on it, increasing the costs of the business.

Taking out a loan could affect its capital structure and turn it into a high-geared business. This means it would be at a higher risk in terms of increases in interest rate.

Share capital might be another way to finance new equipment as this also has no interest payments and does not have to be paid back. Overall, though, retained profit is probably the best way for McNab's.

ⓔ **3/9 marks awarded.** Not only does this answer lack application, the structure in three (rather short) paragraphs limits the development (analysis) of arguments.

(f) Investment into technology is likely to have a big impact on competitiveness. This is because technology can significantly improve the efficiency of production. More can be made in less time from fewer workers. This means increased productivity, costs are lower and the unit cost of production will go down. As a result, prices can be reduced, making the business more competitive.

Investment in technology is also likely to result in an increase in quality and a reduction in wastage. This will perhaps enhance the reputation of the business for quality, making it more competitive and the reduction in wastage will again reduce costs, making it more competitive.

Overall, therefore, it would appear that the investment in new technology is the key to the competitiveness of McNab's.

ⓔ **7/16 marks awarded.** This answer is rather one-sided as it simply addresses how technology might improve competitiveness without any consideration of other factors. There is some development (analysis) and some limited application. The final judgement, however, lacks real support.

(g) On the face of it, this would seem a poor decision by McNab's because demand has fallen and the company is making a loss. Keeping workers who are not needed only adds to the costs of the business and the loss being made. The business could easily lay off some workers and reemploy them when demand picks up, thereby saving the business a good deal of money.

However, it may be that the unions within the business are particularly strong and they do not want to cause problems for the future by upsetting them. It may be this is just an effort to keep the peace between them. Damaged labour relations could cause problems well into the future, so it may be a good decision to not lay off workers.

Overall, though, I believe this was a bad decision as the business is loss-making.

ⓔ **7/16 marks awarded.** Overall, this answer has some balance but it demonstrates a lack of understanding of the underlying issues in the case such as the nature of the product and existing labour relations. There is some relevant development of argument and application in the first paragraph, but the second is not in context and the final conclusion lacks support.

(h) External factors are things such as competition and the economic, political and ethical factors that might affect a business's performance. Internal factors include the resources available and the style of management.

McNab's has been affected by the economic climate and this has caused a fall in sales, leading to a decline in profit. Other factors might be competition, weather, ethical issues. Internally: management style and resources available.

Overall, I believe it was external factors.

e **4/20 marks awarded.** This student was clearly running out of time when answering this final question. This type of answer, with just a series of points, is often seen in exams and something that should be avoided. A list of unconnected points can only ever attain content marks and this student may well have scored more marks if they had focused on developing one point more fully. Even the briefest of argument that has some context will score more marks than a list of points.

e **Total score: 27/80 marks = overall, this response is weak as it lacks application and depth of argument throughout and would struggle to achieve a pass grade.**

Essay questions (A-level)

Question 1

'Numerical data such as market share, market growth and profitability ratios are the best and only way to judge how successful a business is.' To what extent do you agree with this statement?

(25 marks)

Student A

Numerical data is important in judging how successful a business may or may not be, but it is not necessarily the best or only way of judging business performance. a

The objective of almost all businesses is to make a profit and therefore the extent of their profit and improvements in profitability ratios such as operating profit margin are a good indication of success. Other ratios such as return on capital employed and numerical data such as market share also provide an indication of success. However, it is important to recognise that such data need to be viewed critically and not accepted at face value. It may be that profitability ratios are falling, but this need not be an indication of a failing business. It may be that they are failing as a result of a downturn in the economy and as a result all businesses within that market are experiencing difficulties. This suggests that although numerical data may be a good way of judging performance, it needs to be looked at in the context of other factors such as the economic climate, the market and competition. On its own, numerical data may be of little use; it needs to be compared with previous years and competitor data as well as being analysed in the context of the market and economic conditions. b

Success of a business may also be judged in the context of customer satisfaction. Some of the UK utility companies such as gas and electricity achieve high profits but customers feel exploited and are far from happy. In some cases this can lead to future problems. Tesco was the leading supermarket; it still has the highest market share of them all, but consumers have become dissatisfied and moved elsewhere, resulting in a decline in profitability. The reputation of a business, its customer satisfaction and customer retention can be a good indicator of the success of a business. If these are good, it can mean the long-term success of the business even though numerical data such as profitability ratios may be relatively static. c

With increased awareness of ethical issues among consumers, a business's ability to set and achieve ethical targets might be an indicator of success. For companies such as The Body Shop and Innocent Smoothies, ethical issues are important. Not only do they contribute to their success, their success may also be judged by the extent to which they achieve these objectives. It is also likely that trying to achieve ethical objectives will incur additional costs that may reduce the profitability of the business, impacting on profitability ratios. This suggests again that it is not only numerical data that are the best and only way of measuring the success of a business. d

Finally, the success of a business is perhaps best measured in the context of how effective it has been in meeting its corporate objectives. It may be that part of a business's corporate objective relates to profitability, but it is also likely there are other objectives. This might involve breaking into new markets, it might be in terms of innovation or it might be in terms of ethical objectives. Therefore, success in this case needs to be judged in accordance with how far these corporate objectives have been achieved. **e**

Overall, it would appear that numerical data are neither the best nor the only way of judging the success of a business. Reputation and customer satisfaction are also important, as are ethical issues and how well a business does in achieving its corporate objectives such as innovation. For example, Apple may have done well in terms of profitability, but it is its success in terms of innovation that will determine its continued success. **f**

e **a** The first sentence sets out the view taken that will, it is hoped, be supported throughout the essay. **b** This paragraph looks specifically at numerical data and how useful they might be, it is written in the context of the question set, the argument is well developed and it is judgemental. **c**, **d** and **e** The next three paragraphs address other factors that might be used to judge the success of a business, such as customer satisfaction/reputation, ethical issues and whether or not a business achieves its corporate objectives. Again, the arguments are well developed, some good real-life examples are included and there is no doubt that this student is addressing the question set. **f** The final paragraph draws the answer together with the conclusion being fully supported by the answer as a whole.

A well balanced, well planned and well written answer. There is no doubt that this response would achieve a top grade A.

Student B

Numerical data is important in measuring how successful a business has been or is. Profitability ratios such as operating profit margin tell us how much of every pound sold is profit. A 4% margin means 4 pence of every pound sold is profit. If a business can show improvements in this ratio, this indicates a very successful business. **a**

Market share is also an important figure. If a business can increase this, it means it is capturing sales from competitors. This leads to greater revenue and therefore greater profit. Again, this indicates a very successful business, meaning numerical data are a good way of judging success. **b**

In order to be useful, however, numerical data should not be looked at in isolation. It is only possible to judge success if these data are compared in some way, perhaps using a previous year or other companies in the same market. Just because your business has improved its profitability ratios does not necessarily mean it has been successful; if a competitor's ratios and profit have increased by a greater amount, your business may in fact have performed poorly. Figures should also be compared over time. A gradually rising figure would be preferable to an erratic trend, with exceptional years mixed with very poor years. The latter would not be viewed kindly by shareholders as share price and dividend may also be erratic. **c**

Another ratio that might be used to measure success might be the return on capital employed. This compares profit to the amount invested in the business. The higher the percentage, the more successful a business has been and as a result this would be a good measure of success. **d**

Gross profit margin is another piece of numerical data that might be useful in measuring success. This indicates how successful a business has been in controlling its direct costs of production. The higher the ratio, the more successful. **e**

Finally, a business could just look at the profit figure as this gives a good indication as to whether it has performed better or worse than the previous year. As such, it gives an indication of success. **f**

Overall, it does seem that numerical data is the best way of measuring the success of a business. There may be other factors to consider, but at the end of the day it is the profit and numerical data everyone looks at. **g**

e **a** and **b** The first two paragraphs are rather descriptive, showing how profit margins and market share might be used to judge success. **c** The third paragraph begins to question the usefulness of numerical data and there is a reasonable argument running through this with some judgement. However having done this student B now seems to be running out of ideas. **d**, **e** and **f** The next three paragraphs simply outline other numerical measures suggesting they can be used to measure success. **g** The final paragraph simply reaffirms that numerical data is the best way to measure success. Having failed to address any other factors however this answer lacks balance and the conclusion as a result has little in the way of support.

Overall this answer would probably achieve a pass grade but at the lower end, E grade.

Question 2

'Motivation of employees has been the subject of much debate and many theories as to how to motivate employees. However, such theories are worthless in practice as the methods of motivating a particular group of workers will on all occasions vary according to the individual circumstances of the particular business in question.' To what extent do you agree with this statement?

(25 marks)

Student A

Although theories of motivation may have little use in practice, this does not mean to say they are worthless. The fact that motivation has been studied is important in itself and those theorists belonging to the human relations school have emphasised the importance of treating workers as human beings and the requirement of management to satisfy their needs. This was a big change from the scientific school that viewed workers more like machines who were motivated only by money. **a**

No one single theory is likely to be used specifically as a model to improve motivation in an individual business, but looked at collectively they do offer some practical suggestions in terms of motivation. Looking at the theories of Maslow, Herzberg and McGregor, it is possible to identify a number of similarities. Maslow in his pyramid of needs had basic needs at the bottom and self-esteem and self-actualisation at the top. These basic needs relate to the hygiene needs of Herzberg and the self-esteem and self-actualisation relate to the motivators. The motivators put forward by Herzberg were such things as recognition, responsibility, involvement and status — the very characteristics that are likely to be required to achieve Maslow's self-actualisation. McGregor looked at workers from a different perspective, splitting them into X and Y workers. He described Y workers as those who sought recognition, responsibility and involvement and that management should do all they could to provide the circumstances by which this could be achieved. b

From a quick look at these theories, it seems that recognition, responsibility, involvement and status are common denominators. For a workforce to be fully engaged and motivated, it would seem that creating the circumstances where they are recognised, involved in the decision-making process and have responsibility is the key. Looking at the theories from this point of view would seem to suggest that they do have some relevance when it comes to trying to create a fully engaged motivated workforce. c

Of course, the individual circumstances within each business will dictate how this actually takes place. Sometimes it may be achieved by job enrichment, where individual jobs are expanded vertically to give more responsibility. It might be through job redesign, where the role of a worker is completely changed. Sometimes this will be achieved by changing the way work is done, such as the introduction of team-working. All of these are non-financial methods of trying to achieve a greater degree of engagement, motivation and performance within a workforce. The key aspect of each method, however, is that of trying to give workers greater recognition, responsibility and involvement — exactly what the theorists have suggested in their various theories. d

So to what extent are these theories worthless? It is true that it would be unlikely for a manager to try to base any attempt to improve engagement and motivation on an individual theory and from this point of view they are pretty worthless. This does not mean to say they have no role to play. They have highlighted the need to treat workers as human beings who have needs that should be recognised. These needs seem to revolve around the ideas of responsibility, recognition and involvement and it appears that the various methods of non-financial motivation try to address these needs. Overall, although individually such theories may have little worth, collectively they may well have had a big influence in the way workers are motivated. e

e a The first paragraph provides a good introduction to the issue of motivation theories and suggests that, although they may not be used specifically, they do have some worth. b and c The next two paragraphs are excellent. This student has identified a number of common denominators within the various theories, which it is suggested might be used when trying to create a fully engaged and motivated workforce. Although McGregor is not listed in the specification, it is always refreshing to see students demonstrating their wider reading in answers, particularly when this can add to the arguments being made. **d** This paragraph goes on to suggest that the practical non-financial methods of motivation are actually putting into practice the common denominators outlined earlier. **e** Finally, this paragraph draws the essay together with a fully supported conclusion that although the theories may not be used directly, what they are saying collectively has some worth and relevance to business.

Overall, this is a well-considered and carefully constructed essay that would easily achieve a grade A.

Student B

There are a number of theories of motivation that might be used in an attempt to motivate workers. First, Abraham Maslow developed a pyramid of needs ranging from basic needs, physiological and security at the bottom and moving through social and self-esteem needs to self-actualisation at the top. He argued that workers could not move on to the next level until the preceding level had been fulfilled. Frederick Herzberg, on the other hand, developed a two-factor theory where on the one side he had hygiene factors such as pay and working conditions and on the other side motivating factors such as recognition, responsibility and involvement in decision-making. **a**

Maslow and Herzberg belong to what is known as the human relations school where workers are treated as human beings who have individual needs. One of the first theorists was Taylor, who looked at work from a scientific view point — workers were simply an extension of machines. The amount produced could be improved by changing the way work was done and the tools used, so they were best for the purpose. Taylor believed that workers were motivated only by money, so by changing the way they worked to produce more would motivate them as they would be paid more under a piece-rate system. **b**

In practice, businesses may not look at these theories as there are various non-financial means of motivation. Job enlargement and job enrichment may be introduced, where a worker is given more tasks with enlargement leading to a more varied job and with enrichment more responsibility within the job being done. Another way of motivating the workforce might be to introduce team-working, where workers are organised into teams and given control and responsibility over a particular aspect of production. This might include responsibility for ordering parts and quality control. The actual method used depends on the individual circumstances of the business and probably the style of management used. **c** As well as non-financial methods, there are also financial methods of motivation. These include piece rate (payment according to the amount produced), bonuses, profit-sharing and share option schemes. All of these methods might encourage workers to work harder and produce more. **d**

Overall, I agree that the various theories of motivation are worthless in practice. It would be just about impossible for a manager to base any idea for improved motivation on one single theory. What they should do is look at the various financial and non-financial methods of motivation and decide which might be the most appropriate for their particular business. **e**

ⓔ **a** The first paragraph is rather descriptive and lacking in focus on the question — all it does is outline the theories of Maslow and Herzberg. **b** The second paragraph continues in the same vein, this time outlining the work of Taylor. As yet, the question has not been addressed. **c** and **d** These paragraphs seem to suggest that businesses are more likely to use the various methods of financial and non-financial methods of motivation rather than to refer to theories, but this has not been executed very effectively. **e** The final paragraph tries to draw this together, but any support for the view taken is only limited and, overall, this student has struggled to come to terms with this essay.

At best, this response would be likely to achieve a grade E.

Quantitative skills question practice (AS and A-level)

Questions 1 to 3 focus on the operational objectives of labour productivity, unit or average costs of production, capacity and capacity utilisation.

Question 4 tests your understanding of capital structure, capital gearing and return on capital employed.

Question 5 tests your understanding of the various profit margins.

Questions 6 and 7 focus on contribution, break even and margin of safety.

Question 8 addresses the human resource targets of labour turnover, labour retention, unit labour cost, labour costs as a percentage of turnover and labour productivity.

Question 1

From the information below, calculate:

(a) Labour productivity.

(b) Unit (average) cost of production.

Output	7.5m units
Number of employees	250
Cost of production	£2.5m

Question 2

A business has a total capacity of 250,000 and is currently operating at 85% capacity. What is its current production level?

Question 3

A business is currently producing 7.5m units and has a maximum capacity of 9m units. What is its capacity utilisation?

Question 4

From the information below, calculate:

(a) The level of capital gearing.

(b) The return on capital employed.

(c) The change in gearing if borrowing increases to £17m.

Borrowing	£13m
Equity	£15m
Operating profit	£2m

Question 5

From the information below, calculate:

(a) Gross profit margin for each year.

(b) Operating profit margin for each year.

(c) Profit for the year margin.

(d) The percentage change in operating profit.

	2013	2014
Sales revenue	£150m	£160m
Gross profit	£45m	£46m
Operating profit	£14m	£14.5m
Profit for the year	£7.5m	£7.5m

Question 6

From the information below, calculate:

(a) Contribution.

(b) Contribution per unit.

(c) Break-even output.

(d) Margin of safety.

Sales revenue	£160m
Fixed costs	£10m
Variable costs	£135.5m
Output	8m units

Question 7

Using the information for Question 6, calculate:

(a) The new break-even output if fixed costs increase by 10%.

(b) The new break-even output if price increases by 10%.

(c) What impact do the above changes have on the margin of safety?

Question 8

From the information below, calculate:

(a) The labour turnover figure.

(b) The labour retention figure.

(c) Labour costs per unit.

(d) Employee costs as a percentage of turnover.

(e) Labour productivity.

Number of employees	800
Labour costs	£8m
Sales revenue	£14m
Number of leavers	50
Number of workers employed more than 1 year	700
Output	2m units

Answers to quantitative skills question practice

Note that all answers are given to two decimal points and in each case indicate units (for example, m), value (for example, £) or percentage (%). It is essential that you also show these in your final answers. Not doing so could cost you a mark. It is also essential that all working is shown as credit will be given for this. For example, if you make one mathematical error and just put down an answer you will get no marks, but if your workings are there and the calculation is undertaken correctly you might lose only 1 mark.

Question 1

(a) Labour productivity = $\dfrac{\text{output}}{\text{number of employees}}$

$= \dfrac{7,500,000}{250}$

= 30,000 units per employee per year

(b) Unit cost = $\dfrac{\text{total cost of production}}{\text{output}}$

$= \dfrac{2.5}{7.5}$

= £0.33

Question 2

Current production level = 85% of 250,000

$= \dfrac{250,000 \times 85}{100}$

= 212,500 units

Question 3

Capacity utilisation = $\dfrac{\text{actual output}}{\text{maximum possible output}} \times 100$

$= \dfrac{7.5}{9} \times 100$

= 83.33%

Question 4

(a) Level of capital gearing $= \dfrac{\text{loan capital}}{\text{total capital employed}} \times 100$

$$= \frac{13}{28} \times 100$$

$$= 46.43\%$$

(b) Return on capital employed $= \dfrac{\text{operating profit}}{\text{capital employed}} \times 100$

$$= \frac{2}{28} \times 100$$

$$= 7.14\%$$

(c) New gearing $= \dfrac{\text{new borrowing figure}}{\text{new capital employed figure}} \times 100$

$$= \frac{17}{32} \times 100$$

$$= 53.12\%$$

Change in gearing $= 53.12 - 46.43$

$$= 6.69\% \text{ increase}$$

Question 5

(a) Gross profit margin $= \dfrac{\text{gross profit}}{\text{sales revenue}} \times 100$

For 2013:

$$= \frac{45}{150} \times 100$$

$$= 30\%$$

For 2014:

$$= \frac{46}{160} \times 100$$

$$= 28.75\%$$

(b) Operating profit margin $= \dfrac{\text{operating profit}}{\text{sales revenue}} \times 100$

For 2013:

$$= \frac{14}{150} \times 100$$

$$= 9.33\%$$

For 2014:

$$= \frac{14.5}{160} \times 100$$

$$= 9.06\%$$

(c) Profit for the year margin = $\dfrac{\text{profit for the year}}{\text{sales revenue}} \times 100$

For 2013:

$= \dfrac{7.5}{150} \times 100$

$= 5\%$

For 2014:

$= \dfrac{7.5}{160} \times 100$

$= 4.68\%$

(d) Change in operating profit $= 5 - 4.68$

$= 0.32$

Change as a percentage $= \dfrac{0.32}{5} \times 100$

$= 6.4\%$ decline in profit

Question 6

(a) Contribution = sales revenue – variable costs

$= 160m - 135.5m$

$= £24.5m$

(b) Contribution per unit = $\dfrac{\text{contribution}}{\text{output}}$

$= \dfrac{24.5m}{8m}$

$= £3.06$

(c) Break-even output = $\dfrac{\text{fixed costs}}{\text{contribution per unit}}$

$= \dfrac{10m}{3.06}$

$= 3,267,974$ units

(d) Margin of safety = actual output – break-even output

$= 8,000,000 - 3,267,974$

$= 4,732,026$ units

Question 7

(a) New break-even output = $\dfrac{\text{new fixed costs}}{\text{contribution per unit}}$

$= \dfrac{10m + 10\%}{3.06}$

$= \dfrac{10m + 1m}{3.06}$

$= \dfrac{11m}{3.06}$

$= 3,594,771$ units

(b) New sales revenue = 160m + 10%

$\qquad\qquad\qquad\qquad$ = 160m + 16m

$\qquad\qquad\qquad\qquad$ = £176m

$\quad$ New contribution = new sales revenue – variable costs

$\qquad\qquad\qquad\qquad$ = 176m – 135.5m

$\qquad\qquad\qquad\qquad$ = £40.5m

$\quad$ New contribution per unit = $\dfrac{\text{new contribution}}{\text{Output}}$

$\qquad\qquad\qquad\qquad$ = $\dfrac{40.5m}{8m}$

$\qquad\qquad\qquad\qquad$ = £5.06

$\quad$ New break-even output = $\dfrac{\text{fixed costs}}{\text{contribution per unit}}$

$\qquad\qquad\qquad\qquad$ = $\dfrac{10m}{5.06}$

$\qquad\qquad\qquad\qquad$ = 1,976,284.5 units

(c) The change in fixed costs leads to a decrease in the margin of safety and the change in price leads to an increase in the margin of safety.

Question 8

(a) Labour turnover = $\dfrac{\text{number of employees leaving}}{\text{total number of employees}} \times 100$

$\qquad\qquad\qquad$ = $\dfrac{50}{800} \times 100$

$\qquad\qquad\qquad$ = 6.25%

(b) Labour retention = $\dfrac{\text{number of employees employed for more than 1 year}}{\text{total number of employees}} \times 100$

$\qquad\qquad\qquad$ = $\dfrac{700}{800} \times 100$

$\qquad\qquad\qquad$ = 87.5%

(c) Labour costs per unit = $\dfrac{\text{labour costs}}{\text{output}}$

$\qquad\qquad\qquad$ = $\dfrac{8m}{2m}$

$\qquad\qquad\qquad$ = £4

(d) Employee costs as a percentage of turnover = $\dfrac{\text{labour costs}}{\text{turnover}} \times 100$

$\qquad\qquad\qquad\qquad$ = $\dfrac{8m}{14m} \times 100$

$\qquad\qquad\qquad\qquad$ = 57.14%

(e) Labour productivity = $\dfrac{\text{output}}{\text{number of employees}}$

$\qquad\qquad\qquad$ = $\dfrac{2m}{800}$

$\qquad\qquad\qquad$ = 2,500 units

Knowledge check answers

1 Operations management is concerned with converting materials and labour into goods and services in the most efficient manner possible in order to maximise the profit of a business.

2 Environmental concerns impact on operational objectives in terms of the amount of packing used, energy usage and waste disposal.

3 Four reasons for setting operational objectives include they promote efficiency within a business; unit costs may be reduced because of the efficiencies gained; profitability may improve as a result; they can be a means of evaluating performance.

4 Capacity refers to the total or maximum amount a business can produce, whereas capacity utilisation is the percentage of the total capacity it is currently using.

5 Excess capacity is spare capacity — the amount of potential capacity a business is not using.

6 Four ways to improve labour productivity include reduce the labour force without reducing production; invest in technology; improve training; motivation and job redesign.

7 Two benefits of just-in-time production are reduced costs and reduced damage/wastage. Two drawbacks are related to the reliability and flexibility of the supplier so that production is not interrupted and bulk purchase discounts might be lost.

8 Capital-intensive production is where there is a much greater reliance on capital and technology rather than labour, whereas labour-intensive production is where there is a much greater emphasis on labour rather than capital and technology.

9 Competitive advantage refers to an aspect of a product or service that influences a consumer to purchase one product rather than another.

10 Four possible measures of quality include number of complaints; the amount of wastage; no. of returns; punctuality.

11 The attitude of employees can cause difficulties in improving quality as they are often resistant to change and believe their job security may be threatened.

12 Businesses ignore quality at their peril because, once damaged, a reputation can be difficult to recover. Consumers may buy a good once, but they will not return and a damaged reputation will spread quickly by word of mouth and social media.

13 Buffer inventory is the minimum amount of inventory (stock) that a business wants to hold and acts as a cushion against late delivery. Reorder level is the point at which an order for more stock is placed. Reorder quantity is the amount that is reordered each time.

14 Outsourcing may save a business costs, especially if an increase in demand is temporary, and it may mean a quicker response. However, a business may suffer if the quality and reliability of the outsourcing company is not up to standard and outsourcing may be costly.

15 Three benefits of setting financial objectives include they provide a focus to decision-making; they provide a yardstick against which to measure performance; shareholders might use them to analyse a potential investment.

16 Cash flow refers to the money going into and out of a business, whereas profit is the amount left over after all costs have been taken from revenue.

17 The reason operating profit may increase while gross profit remains the same is because a business has been able to reduce its operating expenses.

18 Capital expenditure is money spent on the fixed assets of a business, whereas revenue expenditure is money spent on the day-to-day running of the business.

19 It is important for a business to control its capital gearing ratio because if this increases the business becomes more exposed to increases in interest rates, which not only puts greater pressure on costs but may also reduce consumer spending for some goods.

20 Variance analysis is the study of the reasons for differences between budgeted figures and the actual figures in a budget.

21 Contribution can be used to calculate:

(a) break-even output using the following formula:

$$\text{Break-even output} = \frac{\text{fixed costs}}{\text{contribution per unit}}$$

(b) profit using the following formula:

Profit = total contribution – fixed costs

22 The main problems associated with break-even analysis are that it assumes all production is sold and sold at the same price. It is also difficult to apply accurately to a multi-product firm

23 A trade creditor is someone a business owes money to in the short term (a payable), whereas a trade debtor is someone who owes a business money in the short term (a receivable).

24 The benefits of raising money through equity rather than borrowing are that there is no interest to pay on equity and it does not have to be paid back.

25 If a business tries to shorten the credit period allowed to customers in an attempt to improve cash flow, this could damage relationships as it may be a long credit period that has attracted these customers in the first place.

26 A hard approach to human resource management is where employees are treated as a resource with

little in the way of communication, empowerment and delegation. A soft approach is where there is regular communication and empowerment, and employees are encouraged to take on responsibility.

27 Labour productivity is likely to be affected by the amount of technology employed in production, the skills and motivation of the workforce as well as the external environment such as the state of the economy.

28 Labour turnover refers to the number of employees leaving in a particular time period, whereas labour retention refers to the number of employees who have been with a business for one or more years.

29 It is important to have a fully engaged workforce as this means that employees are likely to be more motivated and productive in the business.

30 The Hackman and Oldham model looks at jobs in terms of five core characteristics (skill variety, task identity, task significance, autonomy and feedback), the impact of these on three critical psychological states (experienced meaningfulness, experienced responsibility for outcomes and knowledge of actual results) and how these in turn influence personal and work outcomes (high internal work motivation, high quality work performance, high job satisfaction and low absenteeism).

31 Hierarchy refers to the levels of work and management within an organisation structure; span of control is the number of subordinates that can be controlled effectively by one manager; delegation is the passing of authority to a subordinate to carry out or manage a task.

32 The style of management uniformity of policy is likely to affect whether a business is centralised or decentralised in that centralisation is more likely with a hard approach to management and a uniform policy, whereas decentralisation may be more likely with a soft approach and non-uniform policy.

33 The main areas covered by human resource flow are recruitment, selection, talent development and dismissal.

34 If a job carries with it a degree of empowerment, involvement in decision-making, responsibility and recognition, it is more likely to lead to engaged employees.

35 The scientific school of management looked at employees as a resource who were solely motivated by money, whereas the human relations school recognised the importance of employees' social needs in motivation.

36 Financial methods of motivation include pay, bonuses, piece rate, commission and profit-sharing. Non-financial methods relate to general working conditions, flexible hours, health insurance and holidays, as well as things such as recognition and involvement.

37 The role of trade unions is to represent their members in their place of employment. This is mainly in terms of pay and conditions of work, but it can include representing an individual in cases of unfair dismissal.

38 The main benefit of good employer–employee relations is that they are likely to result in a more engaged, motivated and productive workforce.

Index